Making Things Work:
Tales From a Cabinetmaker's Life

Nancy R. Hiller

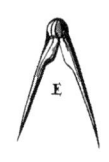

Published by Lost Art Press LLC in 2019
837 Willard St., Covington, KY 41011, USA
Web: http://lostartpress.com

First published by Putchamin Press in 2017
Bloomington, Indiana

Title: Making Things Work: Tales From a Cabinetmaker's Life
Author: Nancy R. Hiller
Publisher: Christopher Schwarz
Copy editor: Megan Fitzpatrick
Design: Meghan Bates
Die Stamp Design: Stephanie Reeves
Distribution: John Hoffman

Copyright © 2019 by Nancy R. Hiller. All rights reserved.

ISBN: 978-1-7322100-8-0

Third printing.

ALL RIGHTS RESERVED
No part of this book may be reproduced in any form or by any electronic or mechanical means including information storage and retrieval systems without permission in writing from the publisher; except by a reviewer, who may quote brief passages in a review.

This book was printed and bound in the United States.
Signature Book Printing, Inc.
8041 Cessna Ave.
Gaithersburg, MD 20879
http://signature-book.com

For my husband, Mark Longacre,
who has tolerated the presence of this badly behaved,
stinking dog beneath the kitchen table
for our 10 years together.

And in memoriam for Kent Perelman,
one of the best and most modest
woodworkers I have known.

Table of Contents

Acknowledgments

1. The English Years

    Living the Dream 3
    The Accidental Cabinetmaker, I 11
    The Accidental Cabinetmaker, II: On the Brink 21
    Get On Your Bike 29

2. Dream On

    A Thing Worth Making, I: Hunting-Badcocke 37
    A Thing Worth Making, II: Hotel California 43
    A Thing Worth Making, III:
    Human Factors Engineering 51
    I Used To Do What You Do 59
    The Excellent Craftsman 65
    No. 73

3. Making Things Work

    Cat and Mouse 95
    Don't Call Me Boss 111
    A Case of Mistaken Identity 115
    The Value of Nothing: A Play in Four Acts 121
    Daniel 129
    It's All Problems 139
    What Price Authenticity? 153

A Note About the Title

Other Books by the Author

Cabinet. 1549. [Eng. Dim. of CABIN, influenced by Fr. *cabinet* – It. *gabinetto* 'closet, press, chest of drawers'.] A little cabin, hut, soldier's tent; a rustic cottage; a lodging, tabernacle; a den of a beast.... A case for the safe custody of jewels, letters, documents, etc.; and thus, a piece of furniture, often ornamental, fitted with drawers, shelves, etc., for the preservation and display of specimens.

Cabinetmaker. 1681. One whose business it is to make cabinets and fine joiner's work.

—*The Shorter Oxford English Dictionary,* 1975

Acknowledgments

For their invaluable encouragement I am grateful to Mary Lee Adler, Lee Sandweiss, Kathryn Lofton, and Mark Longacre.

Edith Sarra and Alexandra Morphet read my draft of an earlier, serious version of this work and provided comments that contributed to my decision to abandon the kind of analysis that might have appealed to two or three readers (and only if they were compelled to read it) and instead create a collection of personal stories enlivened by tongue-in-cheek wit. Alexandra read several of the revised stories and provided comments.

I am grateful to Robert Orsi, for changing the way I see the world, as well as for his patronage and ongoing friendship; Amy Brier, for reminding me that having time for something really important is – at least to a larger degree than many of us acknowledge – a matter of choice (one can always get up an hour earlier, leave the house a wreck, stay at home working instead of taking that vacation, etc.); Sam Ardery, for legal advice on an exceptionally trying job; Robert Meitus, for advice and insight regarding copyright, defamation, and related legal matters; Eric Sandweiss, for the title of one of the chapters, "The Value of Nothing," which comes from an Oscar Wilde quote; Richard F. Busch, for permission to reproduce his photo of my family during the 1960s; Sharon Routen, my accountant, for explaining various matters financial; Jerry Forshee, for introducing me to the term "human factors engineering"; Jim Ferrell, for opening my eyes to the wonder that is Lost Art Press; Megan Fitzpatrick, who copy-edited this work and encouraged me to publish it; Jonathan Binzen, for his editorial comments; Raney Nelson of Daed Toolworks and Crucible Tools, who put me in touch with John Hoffman; John Hoffman, who put me in touch with book designer Meghan Bates and also with Phil Nanzetta of Signature Book Printing, who arranged for printing, binding, and delivery; and Mary Spohn, for advice regarding narrative flow and development. I am enormously grateful to Dan Carlinksy, for reading multiple versions of this material as well as the book proposal, providing important critical remarks, and discussing the project with me by email and phone over a period of years; and to Daniel O'Grady, for making me laugh, for his example as a craftsman, and for his astute remarks on a few of these stories.

A note about identities

These tales are mostly-true. Names and other identifying information have been changed in many cases. One character is a composite of people I have known. My point in writing these tales is emphatically not to insult or offend, but to bring a number of experiences and observations that some of my fellow cabinetmakers and I share into broader conversation. I hope you will find the stories entertaining.

1. The English Years

Living the Dream

"WHY, I CAN'T think of anything in the world better than making furniture in England," said my mother's old friend Bunny, taking a sip of her gin and tonic. It was January 1986 and Bunny was visiting from New Jersey. Knowing that she was going to be in Cambridge for a few days, she'd invited me out for dinner. I rode my bike over to meet her at a pub near her hotel, where I was describing the soul-crushing end of my week.

By this time I'd been working at Farmstead Furniture, a custom cabinetmaking shop, for several months. Earlier in the week my employers had assigned me an elaborate sideboard. I would be building the piece in solid mahogany with hand-cut joinery throughout, trimming the doors and drawer faces with cockbeading fashioned by my own hand, and polishing the piece to a warm luster. It was my most thrilling commission to date.

"Things were going swimmingly," I told Bunny, "until I started gluing the vertical divider into the sideboard's lower section." The divider had a long dovetail at top and bottom that would slide into a matching slot. I brushed glue onto the dovetails and started easing them in. I was about halfway when the divider became too tight to move by hand. This is nothing out of the ordinary; with such a wide assembly there's a lot of friction to overcome, especially as the wood fibers swell from the moisture in the glue. I grabbed my mallet and proceeded to hammer the divider farther into the slot. After a couple more inches it stopped moving. It was a cold day in January; the woodstove, several yards from my bench, was causing the glue to set more quickly than usual. With rising panic I ran over to Stan's bench and grabbed the eight-pound sledgehammer he kept leaning against the wall. Protecting the divider's front edge with a block of scrap, I slammed the sledgehammer against it. The thing wouldn't budge. "Fuck!" I shouted, laying on another blow. Nothing.

"Take this, you fucker." WHAM.

The divider stuck fast. "FUCK!!!" I shrieked at the top of my lungs, hysterical with rage. "*YOU FUCKING PIECE OF SHIT.*" Just then the front door of the workshop opened and one of my bosses, Mike, walked in with an unfamiliar man. "There seems to be a lot of fucking going on in here," he said calmly, casting a distressed look in my direction. "Mind stopping while I show this prospective customer the fine work we do?"

Physically and emotionally drained, I slumped against my workbench and caught my breath. Then I went and got a jigsaw to cut the divider out before making a replacement.

Such misadventure did not go over well at Farmstead. The problem was not so much the cursing, but the waste of time and materials. The business owners kept track of each minute and every scrap of wood. Efficiency was the name of the game. That was the only way to finance what they referred to as their "real" workshop, a purpose-built structure they planned to add on to the former chicken coop that housed their operation. I was ashamed. I should have known better than to fit such a long sliding dovetail so snugly.

"But honey," Bunny remarked, listening to my tale with wide eyes. "You get to do such beautiful work!"

She was right, of course. At Farmstead, each job was truly custom-made, even the kitchen cabinetry. Nothing was built according to standard dimensions; we built to fit the space. When we did a so-called "old-pine" kitchen – they were all the rage at the time – the material really was old pine, salvaged from demolished buildings; the first thing we did was remove the nails. We cut all our dovetails, even for kitchen cabinet drawers, by hand. And although we spray-finished our built-ins, as most shops did, we French polished our furniture. I knew of no other business where I would get paid to indulge my love of traditional techniques and learn more of them.

Of course I had frustrations, foremost among them my ever-present anxiety lest my work fall short of the Farmstead standard. Then there was the matter of my income, so low that a jar of name-brand mustard was a rare splurge. Topping all of this were the routine insults from Aidan, the foreman, a lumbering misanthrope who roamed the shop in baggy shirts and drooping trousers, a put-down for his fellow employees ever at the ready.

"But at the end of the day," I continued as a waiter brought our first course, "I can't deny it. Working at Farmstead is a dream come true." The question remained whether it was the kind of dream that Bunny would recognize.

"OK," Bunny responded, deftly fishing a crouton out of her cream of lettuce soup. "I understand that you have frustrations at work. Who doesn't have the occasional day from hell?! But tell me how you landed such a fabulous job in the first place."

I launched into the back story. A year before, I had fallen hopelessly in love with Gregor Campbell, a classmate during our City & Guilds furniture training in 1979. Back then he'd been an awkward youth of 17. When we reconnected six years later over beer at a pub in Saffron Walden, I was awed by the beautiful man he had become. Six-foot-two, lanky and muscular, with shoulder-length red-blond hair and a beard to match, he literally glowed. Enhancing the allure was his freshly broken heart. I longed to take him in my arms and comfort him. My longing grew more insistent as the evening and beer wore on.

He seemed encouraged by my concern. "Come see our workshop," he said, inviting me to visit Farmstead, where he had worked for several years. "I'll pick you up and take you over," he added, knowing that I still did not drive and that getting there by train would take hours.

The business was housed in a long wooden building surrounded by farm fields. A small addition served as an office, though Stan and Michael, the two partners who owned the place, spent most of their time working alongside their three employees. There was no bathroom; they were all men, the place was in the country, 'nuf said. A shed served as a spray room. Woefully under-insulated, it demanded various weather-related accommodations. Forget about finishing when spring humidity was high or the temperature outside too cold.

Gregor showed me to his bench. He was finishing a blanket chest in quartersawn oak with linenfold carvings in the panels, the whole thing made by hand. The day before he had applied the first few coats of amber shellac. "Looks like a toffee apple," he said self-deprecatingly.

I had never seen such a beautiful object. Solidly built, the carving crisp and astonishingly convincing in its evocation of fabric, the chest, like its maker, radiated a golden glow. Gregor had put so much of himself into it. I realized viscerally for the first time that a handmade artifact is literally an expression of its maker. Lifting the lid, I inhaled the heady fragrance of English brown oak and alcohol, the solvent used with shellac. Gregor's beauty and skill were intoxicating.

Never mind that I was married. My husband, Patrick, and I had been together since I was 17. But now I was falling in love for the first time. It was like being hit by a train.

"Oh my God, that is *so* romantic!" Bunny swooned. "'Like being hit by a train'!"

I broke the news to my husband a few days later: I was at a fork in the road. Only one way led to life. "A psychic at an art fair last summer told me you'd be leaving," he responded, surprisingly resigned to the turn of events.

Unfortunately Gregor soon concluded he did not feel the same way about me. "My mother says I'm not in love with you," he notified me one evening. That night I tossed and turned. When I finally fell into a half sleep around 5 a.m., I dreamed I was a ghostly shade in the underworld. "This is what comes from reading too much Virgil in high school," I quipped to Bunny, trying not to appear maudlin. She had long considered my focus on classics a rare example of worthwhile academic study; obviously this was one case in which my time reading Roman literature had served a practical application.

My mother and sister had moved back to the States a few years before. This was long before the Internet or Skype. Local calls cost a fortune; forget about calling another country. I had no one to turn to. In 10-page letters handwritten on onion-skin paper I poured out my heart to my mother, complete with detailed descriptions of Gregor's chiseled, creamy-white body, so reminiscent of marble statuary. Two weeks later I would receive her reply, always urging me to see the experience as a learning opportunity. "You're projecting your own best qualities onto Gregor," she observed. "What you love in him – the dedication to craft, the long hours, the constant readiness to learn – is exactly what you already possess. You just can't see it."

I resolved to take her advice, tweaking it slightly. If I couldn't be with him, I would do my best to become him – or at least become *like* him. I'd read enough Plato to appreciate the power of eros as a source of motivation. Gregor, at least insofar as he expressed the ideal of the excellent craftsman willing to sacrifice nearly everything for the sake of his work, would be my exemplar.

As it happened, Gregor was ready to expand his horizons. He'd been accepted to study antique restoration at a school whose name our favorite instructor during our City & Guilds training years before had been incapable of uttering without growing misty-eyed. "Stan and Mike need someone to replace me," he said. "I suggested that you could be my replacement. They were dubious because you're a woman. But I told them you're the best female cabinetmaker I know. Obviously I didn't tell them you're the only female cabinetmaker I know!" He chuckled guiltily. I felt like a starving dog loitering around a campfire who'd just been tossed a hush-puppy.

He had called me a cabinetmaker. It was not a title I felt ready to apply to myself. Sure, I'd made my living for a few years in a custom furniture and cabinet shop immediately after my training, but I still didn't feel I could claim the identity implied by that term, *cabinetmaker*. It seemed to demand a depth of professional confidence and existential commitment that I lacked.

I was daunted by Gregor's suggestion that I could replace him. My skills were nowhere close to his. But reconnecting with him had ignited a fire. I arranged an interview with Stan and Mike. Gregor said he'd drive me over and told me to bring a piece of work to show what I could do.

My husband and I had been living in a skinny 19th-century row house in Saffron Walden, one room wide and two rooms deep. Beneath the kitchen was a dirt-floor cellar accessed by a short flight of steps. With scarcely 6' of headroom, the cramped space was illuminated by a single bare bulb. The previous homeowners had left a rickety old wardrobe made of quartersawn oak in a corner of the cellar. I broke the piece apart, set up my folding workbench on the uneven floor, and used my marking gauge, panel saw, and smoothing plane to cut the door panel into a uniform board 1/2" thick by about 6" wide. Squinting in the dim light, I used hardware-store tools – a tenon saw, chisels, and mallet I'd bought when I was 20 – to transform the board into a small dovetailed box with half-blind joints at the front, through tails at the back, and a hinged top. I applied a golden stain, then polished it with amber shellac: my own piece of Gregor.

I accepted the position when Stan and Mike offered. Gregor would be gone, but I would be working in his shadow.

Now I had to find a room somewhere closer to work. "Move in with Jenny," Gregor said during a phone call. "She'd love to have you." Jenny was one of his close friends. She and her boyfriend, Roderick, shared an old row house in Cambridge with three fellow renters. Now that Gregor would be leaving, they needed a new housemate. Jenny, Roderick, and Peter were all 22; the other tenant, Bernice, was a waif of just 18. At 26, I felt positively geriatric.

The place was skanky from the moment you stepped through the front door. The entry hall reeked of stale urine; a pay phone hung on the violent-pink Lincrusta. There was a single bathroom tacked onto the house behind the kitchen; like most old houses in the area, this one had been built without indoor facilities. "What do you do about laundry?" I asked. Jenny told me they washed their laundry by hand in the kitchen sink, threw the sopping mess in a portable spin dryer that Peter had brought with him from Yorkshire, hugged the spin dryer to keep it from jolting across the room, then hung the laundry on the backyard line.

I took the room immediately.

"OK, honey," Bunny interjected, her expression more serious. "Here I draw the line. Skanky and reeking of urine? Why would you move into such a dump?"

"Are you kidding?" I replied. "I was lucky to find a room I could afford in Cambridge, and with friendly people to boot." Of course there was a secret bonus: Here, too, I would be living in Gregor's shadow. In my heartbreak I held fast to that connection.

Every morning I rode my bike to the station in Cambridge and put it in the luggage car on the train to a tiny burg in the countryside, where I got back on the bike to ride the rest of the way to work. Like everyone else, I brought my lunch. I was careful about what I ate and drank because there was no toilet, nor any woods for privacy; the place was surrounded by flat farmland. At the start of lunch break I got on my bike and rode to the village to use the public lavatory, then ate my sandwich in the last few minutes of the half hour. It was fine, though the worsening weather as late summer turned to fall made things harder. As I rode to and from the dank lavatories I tried to see the glowering skies over autumn foliage as dramatic expressions of a Vaughan Williams symphony, rather than the promise of frigid evenings on the railroad platform waiting for the train to take my bike and me back to town.

Although Stan and Mike had not considered a toilet essential[1], they had seen fit to invest in a hot-beverage dispensing machine. A cup of brown liquid labeled "Tea" or "Coffee" could be had at the press of a button for several pence. Every morning at 11 and again, at 4 in the afternoon, Aidan would drag himself through the shop muttering "tea toym," as though with his dying breath. The one thing that cheered him up was seeing that some sexist joke or derogatory comment he'd made about my work got under my skin; then he grinned so wide that his gums showed.

---

[1] They did install one before I left their employ, when they built the shop addition.

It was a graphic display of inadequate dental care.

"She thinks the sun shines out of Gregor's ass," he'd mutter with a smirk if I mentioned his former coworker. Whenever he walked past my bench he'd growl "ROUGH," sometimes yipping like a dog. His comment following news that the space shuttle Challenger had exploded was "Serves 'em right for thinking they could fly." His antics were asinine, and for the most part I shrugged them off. But having his miserable outlook thrown over me daily like a stinking blanket did nothing to brighten my mood.

"Well of course you're depressed," added Bunny, whose glasses had by now entirely lost their rosy tint. "How can you stand to keep working there?"

It was simply the reality of working in a rural English woodworking shop in the mid-1980s. Farmstead had offered me an invaluable opportunity to hone my skills and broaden my horizons. At last I felt I'd grown into the identity connoted by the word "cabinetmaker." For that I was grateful. But by the time the waiter brought our crumble and custard, Bunny understood there might be something better than earning one's living by making furniture in England.

The Accidental Cabinetmaker, I

THE STORY of how I got that fabulous job at Farmstead Furniture has its own back story. It begins with my decision to swap the rarefied halls of Cambridge University for a job at a metal-casting factory in 1979.

I'd gone to Cambridge the year before, thanks to a government grant. I planned to pursue a degree in Hebrew and Aramaic, not because I wanted to go to college (in fact, I was completely burned out academically), but thanks to a sense of obligation instilled by the mother of my dear friend Edith. "Your parents will be so disappointed if you don't go," she'd said over mint tea brewed with leaves freshly picked from her garden. She was unaware that my parents strenuously avoided imposing such expectations, which had straitjacketed their own younger years.

So I dutifully vowed to apply to college, but just one: Cambridge[1]. I'd visited the campus with a cousin when I was in high school and been smitten with the soaring Gothic architecture. I decided I would go if I got in; the odds of my being accepted were so slim that I felt confident I'd be off the hook. When I opened the envelope that brought news of my acceptance, along with an antiquated honor known as an exhibition, I figured there must be some Purpose I was Meant to Fulfill by going.

I approached my studies there with the devotion of a seminarian convinced that she would find God – or at least experience an epiphany regarding the point of college, beyond the basic acquisition of a bachelor's degree (a credential far less important in England at the time than it is in the States today). But there was no epiphany, other than the dishearten-

---

[1] The word "college" is a little confusing here. In the States it is often used as a synonym for "university." In England, especially where Oxford and Cambridge are concerned, a university is the degree-granting institution, while the colleges within it provide room and board, along with personal and ancillary academic support.

ing realization that Cambridge was something of a party school for many of my fellow undergraduates. I had no interest in parties, and as a painfully shy American amid the prevailing atmosphere of entitlement and self-importance, I felt distinctly out of place. I reminded myself that I, at least, was there to immerse myself in *scholarship*. I kept a strict schedule and hewed to a quasi-monastic routine that the glorious architecture seemed to call for. But the whole thing felt appallingly self-indulgent. Why was I there, when I had no desire to teach biblical languages or go on to post-graduate study?

Keenly aware that I was blowing a once-in-a-lifetime shot at the kind of benefits that might accompany a degree from such a prestigious institution, I decided to drop out. I moved back to the flat that my boyfriend and I had called home in a part of London known as Newington Green. Look the place up today and you'll find it billed as a haven of cocktail lounges, European bakeries, and tree-lined streets: a hopping cosmopolitan base for stylish, creative types. But this center of comfort and sophistication was not *our* Newington Green. When we lived there, it was dirty and dodgy. In my memory, the sky, like the rest of the scene, is always gray. Naturally it was just this down-at-the-heels character that attracted us, a couple with near-minimum-wage jobs, simply because we could afford to live there.

Our flat was on the second floor of Congreve House, a hulking brick edifice constructed shortly after World War II in a cluster of government-subsidized residences called an "estate." Each of the buildings was named for a famous British writer. Although I didn't know it at the time, William Congreve was an 18th-century playwright known for his poetry and high-brow satire. But the urine-soaked stairwells, prison-worthy architecture, and minefield of dog turds that passed for a lawn belied any association with such refinement.

Whatever the case, by the time we arrived, Congreve House and its equally improbably named neighbors had been virtually abandoned. The utilities in the vacant flats had been disconnected and their toilets filled with cement to discourage squatters. The borough that owned the estate no longer rented the buildings out, because they were deemed substandard. Luckily for us, they had contracted with a local housing co-op to rent some of the flats to artists and erstwhile students of the humanities. Ecstatic at finding a place for a few pounds a month, we'd signed up immediately and arranged to move in as soon as the loo was operational.

Like any masonry building in the damp chill that is English weather for much of the year (or was, back then), our flat was always cold. A small gas heater in the living room put out enough warmth to make a 5' semicircle in front of it just bearable, but beyond that you were on your own. We used a portable paraffin heater in our bedroom and went back and forth about whether the acrid smoke that permeated our bedding, clothes, and even the paint on the walls was better than shivering all night.[2]

Once this character-building habitation had again become my home, I returned to a clerical job I'd had during the year I took off between high school and university: a temporary position at the headquarters of the Automobile Association, near Leicester Square. My boyfriend, Patrick, was 13 years older than I. By day he delivered commercial floor mats for a national company, but his identity was completely bound up with his avocation as a Celtic artist. He spent his spare time hunched over a drafting table, pen in hand, laying out intricate knot-work borders and images of intertwined mythological beasts. Once he'd penned the outlines in black, he colored them in with paint. He sold these creations for the equivalent of pennies per hour at gatherings populated by latter-day druids and henna-haired vixens.

We had no plan beyond supporting ourselves from one week to the next. So when my mother mentioned that she and my stepfather could rent us the two-up, two-down cottage attached to the old house they'd bought in the village of Friday Bridge, we leapt at the chance to escape.

Patrick had enough contacts in London to keep himself marginally employed as a freelance artist, but I needed a job. Finding employment had never been a problem for me because my expectations were so low. From the age of 15 I'd had a succession of jobs – cleaning flats for widows and divorcées in Golders Green, prepping boiled eggs and tomatoes for the lunch line at the ABC Bakery, selling herbal supplements at Selfridge's,

---

[2]"Enough about the cold," you may be thinking. Yes, the English cold features large in a few of these tales. Sorry about that. It was an inescapable reality in those days, when most buildings where I lived and worked lacked insulation. Did I mention that double-glazed windows were still a novelty? While actual temperatures were relatively mild (it didn't get much below 0° C all that often in the areas where I lived), the air was perennially damp. A friend's mother, who had moved to the U.K. from Manitoba, called England's a "penetrating cold" and swore it was far worse than the dry cold of her homeland, where the temperature could stay below -10° C for weeks. So just be glad you're reading about this kind of cold and not experiencing it.

even hawking personal security alarms door to door in London's garment district – until the culmination of my youthful employment, the job at the Automobile Association, where I sold maps, international driving permits, windscreen defrosters, and sunglasses that tinted themselves automatically on those rare occasions when the sun emerged from behind the clouds.

"You could probably get a job at HighQual," said my mother, shortly after we arrived in Friday Bridge late that spring. HighQual was a metal-casting factory a few miles away; my mother knew about it because one of her friends had suggested she contact the owner regarding some hard-to-find sculpting material. I rode my bike over and was hired on the spot for an entry-level position.

HighQual specialized in cast metal parts for industrial and military equipment. The place was steamy, the air loud with the growl and hiss of motors and pneumatic lines. Other workers chatted as they soldered and polished, but I was too nervous to talk. This was before today's paternalistic safety technologies; a moment's inattention could mean a second-degree burn from molten wax or a hand lost to an automated platen. One afternoon a blood-curdling shriek tore through the din when a young woman, distracted by conversation, forgot to move her hand in time to keep two fingers from being crushed. Frantic activity surrounded her as she fainted and was carried off to the hospital. I thought I would never get the sound of her scream out of my head.

Nevertheless, I felt considerably more at home in the factory than I had at Cambridge. The just-get-on-with-it ethos of my new workplace was refreshing. I studied the blue-collar culture with special interest in the break room, where employees discussed the merits of new cars over piping mugs of tea and *The Sun*, with its daily topless model on page three. No doubt my sense of comfort owed much to a vague awareness that I had alternative options, at least potentially, which freed me from having to make any real commitment to my situation. Predictably, it didn't take long for me to start wondering how my fellow workers could bear the sameness of the days that stretched endlessly before them.

Meanwhile, Patrick and I had almost no furniture. We slept on a piece of bulk upholstery foam and used another as a couch. An empty crate made a coffee table and we rounded out our household with an old chair that Patrick had brought to our relationship. We dined at a small gate-leg table and wooden chairs that my mother had bought at a junk shop. What books and LPs we had were stacked on boards with brick supports.

Between his pay from commissions and mine from the factory, we had just enough to cover basic expenses. There was certainly nothing left over to buy furniture. So I decided to build some. Every field in the drained marshland around us was bordered by ditches that one or more neighbors found handy for disposing of soiled mattresses and other unwanted objects. While riding my bike to and from the factory I occasionally spotted a three-legged table or a chest of drawers that had fallen victim to someone's drunken rage. I would return on foot or ask my mother or boyfriend for a ride to pick these things up, drag them home, and break them down to use for raw material.

I had no woodworking experience to speak of. I'd watched the hippie carpenters who lived with my family when I was 10 and 11 as they built a variety of simple shelters in our backyard. I admired their ability to come up with a design and turn it into a real-life dwelling, however basic. But I hadn't actually learned any skills by watching them. A couple of years later I took woodworking classes at boarding school, but those projects were free-form – salad bowls and toys carved with a mallet and gouges – and did not require the use of a saw and square. I still had no idea how to cut a straight line. "So what?" I figured. "Who needs straight lines?" We just wanted some furniture. Using Patrick's old saw and hammer, and employing our small dining table as a bench, I put together a crude pine bookcase over the course of two weekends.

My stepfather stopped by regularly. No visit was complete without some insult directed at my efforts. "Cor, Nance, what are you?", went the usual refrain, a question he invariably answered, himself, with a spirited "Useless." Judging by how often he engaged in this routine, it seemed to give him considerable pleasure. One day he added "you should take a carpentry course" to the standard insult. To spite him, I decided to do just that.

I rode my bike over to the vocational college in Wisbech, a town about three miles away, and arranged to meet with the head of the woodworking department. Mr. Pearce was a kindly man in a white shop coat. "So you want to take a carpentry course, do you?" he asked, eyebrows raised. "What do you intend to do with that?"

"I want to make things for our house. You know, furniture," I answered.

"Oh, goodness," he replied with a smirk. "You mean furniture making, not carpentry." He showed me around the workshop.

The tuition was readily affordable. England still had a furniture industry in the late 1970s, so there was a healthy demand for training. I would spend several hours each day in classes, then make simple pieces of furniture in my spare time to help pay the rent. I gave my notice at HighQual two weeks before the start of the autumn term.

As a 20-year-old woman in a class of 16- and 17-year-old boys I was something of a freak. Some of my fellow students were already employed by furniture factories, which covered the cost of their training; a foundation in traditional handcraft was thought to yield a better class of foreman or manager, even in a modern factory dominated by industrial machines.

Most of my classmates had a head start: They'd taken woodworking classes at school or grown up helping their fathers with carpentry projects in the evenings. My own father's idea of a good end to the day had been to smoke a bowl of Borkum Riff while nursing a glass of rum and perusing *The New Yorker*, a box of Triscuits at his side. Before he left his career in public relations and became a freelance consultant, he'd dutifully followed the path to success prescribed by his parents, who'd come to New York from Poland in search of a better life. After college and law school he did a stint in the U.S. Coast Guard, married my mother, and moved to Florida, where my mother's family lived. There he began his career.

My maternal grandparents were first-generation Americans born to immigrants from Lithuania and that long-contested region sometimes claimed by Austria, sometimes by Germany, who had settled near New York. They migrated to Miami Beach in 1937, a few years after my grandfather was summoned home from medical school in Glasgow due to the Great Depression. He went on to become a successful hotelier. They raised their daughter to achieve the female version of 1950s success: marriage to a man with a well-paid white-collar job. She'd wanted to study fine arts, but they forbade it; too bohemian. Instead, she studied English and history, met my father during her junior year of college, married him after graduation, and became a homemaker in suburban South Miami.

My mother's version of homemaking differed from that of her friends, most of whom spent their afternoons playing tennis at the country club and driving daughters to Girl Scouts, horseback riding lessons, or ballet. In addition to cooking, sewing clothes, and making butterscotch Jell-O, she turned her artistic vision to transforming her surroundings. "Mother gave me the electric drill for a birthday present when we moved into this house five years ago," she told a reporter for the lifestyle section of a local paper. The story's text was arranged around an eye-catching black-and-white photo of my youthful mother in a striped tank top, hair pulled back, smiling as she used a wire-brush attachment in her drill to strip paint from a salvaged baluster spindle. "The kitchen cabinets had sliding doors, which we didn't like. So I took off the doors, trimmed them down and put them on hinges." Next she changed the kitchen faucet and built us a backyard playhouse. Although she was self-taught and didn't make a point of including me in her projects, her example made an impression. We were in awe of her mechanical abilities. She was the tool user in our family.

This vision of the good life was blown out of the water by the 1960s. As we neared the decade's end, my parents were spending several hours each weekend at a park overlooking Biscayne Bay, where my mother played volleyball while my father gazed into his friend Diane's exposed navel, remarking that he wished he could crawl inside it. Shortly thereafter, my mother took off on a cross-country odyssey of self discovery. By the time she returned, it was clear that their marriage was over. She wanted my sister and me to experience something other than middle-class American culture. Her parents, ruing what they saw as her life's implosion, offered help, exchanging their financial support for the deed to our parents' house. They had good friends in London. My mother, sister, and I moved there in the summer of 1971, arriving just before my 12th birthday.

My sister and I were packed off to boarding school. Our mother enrolled in a fine arts program at Hammersmith College. There she met a much younger man, Joe, who later became our stepfather. A painter and sculptor, Joe had a variety of building skills that he utilized to make a living. After they graduated, he and my mother teamed up as self-employed remodelers. The flexible nature of the business gave them more time to pursue their artwork than they would have had in professional jobs. When I was in high school they commandeered me on weekends to help them transform a series of old row houses in Islington into studios where they could live while working on their etching, painting, and sculpture. But even then, my stepfather seemed to find it more rewarding to make fun of my ineptitude than to explain how I might produce the results he was after.

The glaring disparity between my skills and those of most of my fellow students in the vocational school's furniture making classes just magnified my sense of incompetence. So I felt a certain *schadenfreude* when the bench room, normally quiet, rang with an angry reproach directed at some unfortunate fellow: *"Pirtle! What are you doing to that plane iron?"* or *"Spratt! Stop! You're about to cut off your finger!"* At least I wasn't completely alone.

It was only my determination to make my stepfather eat his words that got me through the year-long training. During the first week I spent two whole days trying over and over to cut a simple lap joint with a saw, chisel, and mallet. Overwhelmed by frustration, I felt my face flush as tears filled my eyes. I hid behind my workbench, pretending to look for a tool on the lower shelf. I was clearly not cut out for this kind of work; I belonged in the world of writing and books. I should forget about learning to make furniture. But as I squatted behind my bench contemplating my options, it occurred to me that the prospect of admitting defeat to Joe was even worse than that of persevering in my effort to cut a straight line. By the end of that day I had made my first well-fitted lap joint.

The City & Guilds curriculum of the time focused heavily on traditional handwork skills. Even before the lap joint, we had learned to use hand tools to transform a rough plank into a workable piece of lumber with two flat faces and edges that were straight, square, and parallel, the kind of board commonly identified as "S4S" (square on four sides) that you might find shrink-wrapped at an indoor lumberyard today.

The main room was laid out with 10 or so workbenches, each long enough to accommodate two benchmates. A pair of doors separated the bench room from a larger room filled with industrial machinery, most of it manufactured in Great Britain. Only after we had learned to flatten and square up a board by hand were we allowed to use the machines to perform the equivalent labor. When the machine room was in use it was deafeningly loud, with a daunting atmosphere of purposeful activity. I made a point of visualizing my fingers running into the blade every time I prepared to press an on switch to remember to keep my hands away from those areas.

Each weekday I rode my bike to and from the college. Between November and May there was no escape from the cold. I wore two pairs of socks covered by plastic bags inside my work boots, imagining that the bags would provide insulation. Instead, I later learned, they hastened tissue damage by trapping moisture. Invariably when I got to school my toes were throbbing, and my fingers shot with pain as the flesh revived in the warmth of the workshop. Despite this daily revival, my toes turned purple and my fingers took on a reddish cast that lasted all year. I discovered that this precursor to frostbite had a name: chilblains. To this day, my fingertips tingle at the first hint of fall's approach.

Following the basics we moved on to more challenging joints. After mastering each technique we practiced on projects that were part of the syllabus: a mirror frame, a coffee table, a dovetailed tool chest, a small box for papers. As we learned more refined techniques – veneering, marquetry, turning, reeding, fluting, and French polishing – we graduated to an elegant two-drawer tabletop chest for storing silverware, and ended the year with a late-1970s interpretation of a Regency-style coffee table. When my sister saw the final project she called it "magnificent," and I realized how far I had come.

By this time I had turned 21 and was ready to start my own business. The fact that I knew nothing about running a business was irrelevant. I was determined. Besides, I needed a break from my live-in relationship. I put a classified ad in the local paper in search of a workshop with living space, imagining people flocking to my door with orders for custom work.

Things did not go quite according to plan.

The Accidental Cabinetmaker, II: On the Brink

DUNCAN DAVIS and Raymond Green had been friends for 20 years, ever since they'd met as students at the Slade School of Art in London. Duncan had moved to Wisbech, drawn by its tranquility and the faded elegance of its historic architecture. He purchased a Georgian house on the river and was restoring it in his spare time. Duncan made a living somewhere between the fine and decorative arts: applying decorative finishes to furniture, hand-lettering ornate business signs, and painting reproduction Canalettos for London patrons.

Raymond, too, had a fondness for old buildings and furniture; he had spent some time restoring and dealing antiques but had finally decided to veer off in another, he hoped more profitable, direction. Artistic country kitchens by Smallbone of Devizes had made a splash in the English press, and it was clear that custom kitchens represented a new area of creative enterprise offering a realistic prospect of making a living.

Raymond had started a kitchen design business, using a storefront in London as a salesroom. Because production would be more economical in a small town, he'd bought a house near Duncan's and converted the stables into a workshop. He furnished the ground floor of the main wing with used industrial equipment and old workbenches. In the center was a woodstove, the heat-source for the two-story building, which had drafty windows and, I'm pretty sure, no insulation. The upper floor would eventually become a bench room with space for cabinet assembly, but for now it functioned as a frigid atelier for Duncan, who spent his days working beside the north windows bundled in layers of overcoats and fingerless gloves.

One day at teatime in the damp basement kitchen of Raymond's house Duncan came across a classified ad in the local paper. "Look at this, Ray.

Someone wants a workshop."

Raymond's ears perked up. He had a workshop – one attached to his house, a mere two rooms of which he regularly occupied, and only while visiting from his home base in London.

The ad was mine. I had recently completed my City & Guilds training and determined that it was time to set myself up in business, preferably in a new living situation away from Patrick. Raymond called to get a better idea of what I was looking for, then followed up with a visit to view my portfolio. Immediately aware that he was dealing with someone whose dreams exceeded her grasp of reality, he proposed a slightly different arrangement from the one I had envisioned: I could use the workshop, but instead of renting it for my own business, which I hadn't yet established, wouldn't it make sense to build a commission for him, one he'd already lined up? The job was for a customer in London. Her base cabinets were made, but the part-time employee who had built them also worked as a milkman; he could only come to the workshop after delivering his last foil-topped bottle of the day. It would take him forever to complete the commission, and the customer was ready for her kitchen to be finished.

He showed me a drawing of a shallow upper cabinet called a "dresser," after the 19th-century kitchen dressers that had inspired the design. Made from clear Baltic softwood, the piece would have a lovely mix of open display spaces and concealed storage. There would be little doors hung on traditional brass butt hinges, a row of spice drawers reminiscent of antique apothecary chests, custom-made bead board, scrollwork friezes, and Roman arches atop decorative split-turned posts. Crowning the ensemble would be a cornice. The proportions and details were beautiful. We scheduled an appointment for me to look at the house and workshop.

On my first visit I appraised the realities of what working there might actually mean. The place would be freezing in winter. I would arrive before Duncan each morning (he *was* an artist), so it would be up to me to empty the woodstove of ash and light it afresh. There was something earthy and poetic about this task, at least as I contemplated it in the abstract on a pleasant autumn day. I imagined myself in romantic terms, rather like a female version of Lady Chatterley's gamekeeper. I could handle this.

Thanks to my year at the vocational college, I was familiar with the bicycle ride from Friday Bridge, four miles from Raymond's workshop. In winter the narrow country roads were dark well before 5 p.m. The route wound through small villages with picturesque names such as Elm and March, islands of human habitation floating in a sea of farmland. Summer meant strawberries; winter, Brussels sprouts. By February or so the air was thick with the sulfurous stench of the sprouts' rotting spires, picked clean of their tiny cabbages. For a few months each year this ride was heaven. But my time at the college taught me that winter was a season to be endured, at least for those of us on bikes; performance fabrics, had they even been invented, would have been well beyond my budget. It was one thing to grin and bear such discomfort for a limited period while I was in school. But now I would be in it for the long haul. High on the prospect of adventure, I decided that the satisfactions of working at Raymond's shop would easily outweigh any physical discomforts the job entailed. Besides, if I was renting a room at his house, I wouldn't have to bike to work each day; I would only need to make that trip on visits home.

I was eager to take Raymond's drawing from two-dimensional representation to real, working object – an object that would bring daily pleasure to Mrs. Rose Connor of Fulham, whose name was on the page. Even though I had never met Mrs. Connor or visited her house, I relished the feeling of personal connection that would be forged between us simply by virtue of her daily use of the cabinetry I was going to make. She would be the recipient of my first professional work, which would become an integral part of her home. I would give the piece my all, building it with loving care, incorporating the best craftsmanship I had cultivated during my training.

On Sunday evening, having installed myself onsite with a change of work clothes, a blanket, some kitchen things, and a few groceries, I made my customary vegetable stew for supper and engaged in a bit of awkward conversation with Raymond. Sharing a house with my new landlord and potential employer was discomfiting for its fusion of intimacy and distance. A native of London's East End, about 20 years my senior, Raymond was married to a respected designer of retro clothing. Blessed with an enviable freedom from self doubt, he quickly became an expert in every venture he embarked on. His cosmopolitanism highlighted my own idealism and naïveté. He indicated that he was skeptical of my desire to flee my domestic relationship. Not knowing how to respond, I filled my hot-water bottle and retired to bed after washing the dishes.

The damp house induced a chill bone-deep. That in itself was unremarkable; the temperature at home was nearly as low, but there, at least,

Patrick and I had a small gas heater in each room to provide a focused source of heat. There, too, I'd had Patrick, a handy source of warmth at night. No way would I be able to undress here; I needed every layer and was not about to sacrifice the fragile aura of heat beneath my clothes in exchange for a bath.

"In fact," I thought, "I'll put on my coat for extra insulation." I got into bed wearing it.

I found it to be no ordinary bed, at least, for the 1980s. Instead, it was a horsehair mattress on worn-out springs. Like old-fashioned British toilet tissue (a euphemism for a completely unabsorbent material resembling thin waxed paper), horsehair beds had long before been superseded by superior modern counterparts. But this room was rarely used, and I was fortunate to find a bed at all. The thin mattress sagged and poked me with bristles whenever a sleepless turn exposed a bit of skin. It had stood so long in this unheated room that it, too, seemed desperate for warmth.

Despite the coat, blankets, and hot-water bottle, I could not relax. I lay awake all night. As dawn broke I noticed a thin layer of fog rolling into the room through a gap between the window frame and the lower sash. So much for the romance of living in a Georgian house overlooking a river.

No matter how I tried to see my new life as an inspiring adventure, the inescapable cold left me emotionally drained. I didn't bathe the entire week; the thought of removing my clothes was unbearable. Nothing adjusts perspective as smartly as severe physical discomfort. On the seventh day I called Patrick and begged him to let me come home. Shaking uncontrollably, I sat in the living room chair by the gas flame. It took hours for the shivering to stop. The rigors of my bicycle commute were nothing compared to the misery of trying to sleep in that room on the North Brink. Not long after that, Patrick and I got married.

At the end of my first week Raymond drove up from London, where he worked on weekdays, to check on my progress. When he found me sanding one of the doors by hand, his face was gripped by anguish. "You can't sand this stuff by hand!" he cried. "That's why we've got an electric sander!" Taking in the rest of the situation – the pre-cut parts, the backsaw, the marking and cutting gauges – he announced that there would be no hand-cut dovetails, either. Nor any lovingly hand-rubbed finish. I was to get over what he called my honeymoon period and use the freestanding dovetail machine, an industrial relic that shook the floor, then spray the finished cabinets with lacquer after staining them. "If you're going to work here, you're going to have to use modern techniques," Raymond declared.

"But you said you wanted my best work!" I blurted in disbelief, considering my best to be the work in which I invested myself most deeply: hands, heart, and mind.

"Look," he said. "It's not about you. It's about the customer. People don't care how things are made; they just want them to be *pretty*."

By the end of the project Raymond was pleased with my work and offered me a job with regular pay at a modest hourly rate.

And thus I became an employee, grateful to have been saved from my naïveté.

As a businessman, Raymond insisted that anything made in his workshop be not only attractive and well constructed, but profitable. He missed no opportunity to point out unnecessary movements or breaches in what he hoped would become a model of efficient production. Each step of the manufacturing process must be standardized – not only the dimensions of parts, such as case sides, tops, and bottoms, or face and door frames, but also the joinery methods. Casework would come in a basic range of sizes so that multiples could be prefabricated and kept ready to assemble when orders came in; any cabinets that deviated from these standards would command a custom charge. He taught me to repeat a given process until all the necessary parts for an order had been made before moving on to the next, because every time I switched from one activity to another I would have to think – and that would take time.

Shortly after he hired me, Raymond began to grow the business. Soon there were three employees, then more, along with a creeping division of labor. I was lucky to be given the job of making dressers, which I found rewarding because of the relative variety. But I soon learned that I could build only so many before I needed some form of mental diversion to keep from feeling suicidal due to the repetitive nature of the work.

Adding to my malaise was my growing appreciation that I was just one small part in the process whereby our customers redid their kitchens. Other people did the selling and design. Still others managed delivery and installation. Without any real say in where the business was headed or what kind of work I might be asked to do in a month, let alone a year, I felt little sense of agency.

It wasn't long before the sheer number of commissions we had to work through undermined that original connection I had felt with Mrs.

Connor. Now the names on shop drawings simply represented abstract customers who distinguished themselves by being pleasant or painful to deal with – and this at several removes. Those who wanted some customization of the basic design were the most appealing; they broke the monotony of my days. The worst were those who changed their mind after I had started their job; it was soul destroying to abandon pieces in which I had already invested so much care, only to redo the work.

On the other hand, one clear benefit of repetitive work is that it offers opportunities for reflection. I wondered why I had ever imagined a connection with Mrs. Connor. We'd never actually met. Raymond was the intermediary between us, so our relationship existed only in my head. Then again, she appeared to share my sense of connection; she had written me a thank-you note after her kitchen was finished. That felt like evidence of a relationship. And there was surely much of me in her cabinets. Several weeks after her kitchen was finished, Raymond took photographs and gave me an 8 x10 print. Now I knew the kinds of things she stored on the shelves, and I was certain that she got great pleasure from this object I had made. I pictured her removing a mug from the lower shelf each morning for tea, or shutting one of the little doors with a satisfying thunk after putting away her dishes. Sure, anyone with equivalent skills could in principle have made her dresser, but I was the one who had actually brought it into being. Beyond this knowledge of brute fact, there was a particularity involved, a craftsman's recognition that had the dresser been made by anyone else, it would have been different: the doors cruder or more refined in their fit, the dovetails (at least, those I'd made before I was forbidden to cut them by hand) looser or tighter. Someone else would have matched the grain differently. He or she might have paid less attention to removing machine marks from the tiny decorative beading worked into the front edges of the shelves. Even if such details might escape the notice of most customers, they are marks by which we, as craftspersons, distinguish ourselves not just from other artisans but individually, *to ourselves*. They are lasting evidence of our skills and care. More than this, they are proof that even if we have been laboring under the weight of routine, even if we are working on the hundredth version of some basic pattern, we have developed a degree of self-discipline that enables us still to care about the quality of the things we make.

I reminded myself daily that I should be grateful to have a job, and one that was far more interesting than those I'd had up to then. But I was deeply unhappy. My romantic vision of furniture making had collided with the realities of doing business in a capitalist economy, or at least Raymond's version of it. In two years I had become despondent. I felt like part of a machine. As long as I had found the work rewarding for its intrinsic satisfactions and the sense of purpose I enjoyed as a craftsperson helping to furnish the kitchens of people with whom I felt some connection, I considered the low pay and often-challenging bicycle commute trivial. But once the work lost that meaning it became increasingly difficult to see myself continuing as a cabinetmaker. Finally I sought refuge in the sociability and sheer physical comfort of office work.

Get On Your Bike

SHORTLY AFTER I left Raymond's employ, Patrick and I moved to Reading, west of London, where I worked in a travel agency for a couple of years. I still built pieces for our home in my spare time, setting up my portable Black & Decker Workmate in the dining room. From there we moved to Saffron Walden, where I reconnected with Gregor, who arranged for me to work at Farmstead Furniture.

By the time I quit my job at Farmstead at the end of 1986, Patrick and I had divorced. I decided to move back to the States. I was 27 and had been in England 16 years. My sister had returned to the States first, my mother, a few years later. I was feeling the need to live on the same land mass as the rest of my family.

Arranging for the move and shipping what possessions I had would take a while, so I needed a temporary job. I went to the Cambridge Job Centre to look for one.

Job Centres were government-operated employment agencies intended to help people find gainful work instead of spending their days watch-ing telly while sponging off the dole. At least, such was the image of their unemployed compatriots entertained by many supporters of Margaret Thatcher, prime minister at the time. Her cabinet ministers (well, some of them) were less dismissive regarding the plight of their jobless constituents. There were jobs out there, they insisted; you just had to put some effort into finding one. "Get on your bike" became an oft-heard exhortation after Norman Tebbit, Secretary of State for Employment, told attendees at the Conservative Party Conference in 1981 that he'd grown up in the 1930s with an unemployed father. "He didn't riot," Tebbit said; "he got on his bike and looked for work and he kept looking 'til he found it."[1]

---

[1] Speech to the Conservative Party Conference, October 1981

The Job Centre certainly made it more convenient to find employment. But I would have found a job with or without it. I was raised by parents who, despite the haziness of their hippie years, impressed on me the importance of hard work and self-reliance. At the same time, they also supported the provision of social services and safety nets, knowing that things can go wrong for anyone, despite diligent work and the best-laid plans.

My friend Beatrice, on the other hand, had graduated from Cambridge with a degree in drama. Finding herself unable to secure paid employment in her field, she didn't hesitate to sign up for the dole. "But surely you could get a job at a sandwich shop, or cleaning houses?" I offered, shocked that this bright, resourceful, relatively well-off friend had sought government assistance.

"If I take a job unrelated to my area of expertise it will count against me the next time I apply at a theatre," she explained over Lapsang Souchong in her cozy London flat. Seeing my stunned expression, she added that taking just any job "would suggest that I'm not serious about my profession."

"Carpenter's assistant," read the card on the rack at the Job Centre. I pulled it down and carried it over to a clerk, who called the museum and arranged for an interview. I'd finally learned to drive the winter before, and had purchased a used Ford Escort van. So the museum's location some 18 miles from where I was living would not be a problem.

I was shocked to learn a couple of days later that I'd been hired. Carpenter's assistant at a military museum? It was still the 1980s. Sexism, at least in many British woodworking shops, was alive and well. And it was still common for me to get angry looks from random men who considered all branches of the building trades their own. "You're takin' our jobs," they'd say. "We've got families to support."

Such remarks left me feeling a sting of guilt. But any sense that I was violating some genuine moral code bound up with gender was fleeting. "Gosh," I wanted to say. "What about me? No one is supporting me. Am I not entitled to support myself? I thought that was part of being a responsible adult."

So I'd been fully prepared to have my application rejected on the grounds that I was, for one reason or another, unsuitable for the position.

The museum occupied a sprawling campus of one-time military buildings, aircraft hangars, and a huge primary exhibition structure. A mind-boggling variety of aircraft spanning the history of aviation was on display, starting with the flimsiest conveyances engineered from balsa wood and fabric. Most impressive to me was a B-series plane that visitors could enter via a ramp. Clambering into its belly one day, I had an epiphany: The planes in which I crossed the Atlantic to visit my family were really no more than cylinders of sheet metal held together with rivets. A horrifying thought. Those molded plastic panels on the sides and ceiling that gave such a comforting sense of sturdiness? They're simply hiding mechanical parts and insulation. I realized that their most important function was to present the illusion that, as my fellow passengers and I sat in our seats watching *Crocodile Dundee* or *Inspector Clouseau*, there was something more substantial between us and the 35,000-foot drop to the ground than a patchwork of aluminum something like 1/8" thick. I pictured the airmen who had once crowded into this plane, weighed down by gear, stinking from days or weeks without a bath, wondering whether they would survive long enough to get home.

Most of the time I worked with George, the head carpenter. A pale man, most likely in his 50s, George always wore a white shop coat over a button-down shirt and neatly ironed trousers. We made display cases, stands for literature, plywood museum signs, that sort of thing. Every so often one of the aircraft restoration crew members needed a part for a vintage wooden plane – say, a hand-shaped propeller blade. Had I stayed there long enough, George and I might eventually have fought over such treats like sharks vying for a bag of pilchards tossed into a tank at the National Aquarium. As it was, though, George pegged me right away as a bleeding-heart Yank he could tease with impunity. By this time I'd been depressed for more than a year and was desperate for some warmth and kindness. We slid into the kind of rapport you see between dogs when a pup is introduced to an established alpha. He didn't just tolerate me; he used me for sport, and I was happy to play along. No sooner would I bend over to saw a small piece in my vise than he'd grab whatever board might happen to be lying around, positioning it like a bat about to whack my ass. No one was watching; no one was poised to capture these moments on film – or on a phone, as they would today. It was just his idea of fun. I was fully aware of his antics, which were stupid and harmless.

Aside from the rare urgent deadline, the pace was relaxed, at least compared to anything I'd experienced at shops in the private sector. I often had to visit other buildings to get measurements or discuss specs, which gave me a chance to explore the campus and familiarize myself with some of the exhibits.

By far the best thing about the job was the break room, where about a dozen of us from different departments gathered each morning around half-past 10, then for lunch at one, and again, later on, for tea. An industrial-size kettle sat on the stove; a roster indicated who would be in charge of making tea before the others arrived. On my first day, George told me how much tea to throw in the pot and how high to pour the water when the kettle boiled. There was always a bottle of milk in the fridge and a bowl of sugar nearby.

The men would stroll in, pour themselves a cup of tea, and take their customary places. Aside from two younger fellows, most of them appeared to be in their 50s or 60s and coasting toward retirement. The break room sped them on their way like one of those moving sidewalks at the airport.

Most of them were married. Their wives packed their lunches, wrapping sandwiches in neat paper or plastic bags, tucking in a packet of crisps alongside some radishes or carrots from the garden. They'd pop in some other little treat – a couple of chocolate digestives, a small container of fruit cocktail, a slice of leftover Madeira cake from a picnic with the grandkids. It seemed clear that most of these men were well cared for and well trained. And because they were expected to behave themselves at home, they leapt at the chance to have some fun with the 27-year-old temp.

"Ah," Eddie would say, peering into his lunch bag. "Let's see. She's packed me a piece of fruitcake. Not my favorite type of cake, but then again, I'll take fruitcake any day over navy cake." I had no idea what navy cake was, but it featured regularly in break room conversation. Everyone around the table would snicker and glance my way. My blank expression just made them chuckle harder; sometimes one or two of them got tears in their eyes. I inferred that navy cake was code for anal sex. Seeing that they found my cluelessness so entertaining, I was glad to play the part of the dumb Yank.

"Passion fruit yogurt," someone else would remark, pulling a small plastic pot from his lunch bag; they pronounced "yogurt" the English way: "*yoggurt*." "Hmm. I wonder whether the wife's trying to tell me something." All eyes would turn to me. I would be the good feminist in the room and avoid taking the bait.

The less I reacted, the higher they ratcheted the inappropriateness. "Now that's something I wouldn't mind being," said Tony one day. He gazed into the distance as though in reverie, then finished his thought: "a saddle on a lady's pushbike," this being Brit-speak for "bicycle."

I shrieked with surprise, then burst out laughing. A small, quick-witted man who always wore a boiler suit over his street clothes, Tony was by far the most outrageous of the lot. I was not offended by the graphic allusion; any man with such a fond appreciation of female genitalia was fine by me, and certainly far more acceptable than one who considered women sexual objects for his own gratification.

Sometimes the phone on the break room wall would ring during lunch. These calls were invariably from Mr. Ladyman, a member of the museum's administration staff whose pasty complexion and rounded shoulders suggested a certain lack of vigor. To compensate, he found it necessary to intrude on our lunchtime fellowship, keenly aware that those with manual jobs considered their break times sacred. Obviously you had to be a twat to expect a man to work when he was off the clock. Some senior member of the crew who knew he really ought to take the call would relent after about a dozen rings. He'd push his chair back from the table and amble slowly over to the phone, muttering "Please call back after fourteen-hundred hours." Of course, when he lifted the receiver, he became the soul of smarmy respectability. "Hello, Mister Ladyman. And what can we do for you today?"

One of the higher-ups left his copy of *The Daily Mirror* in the break room most mornings after our crew had returned to work. At lunchtime, a few of the men passed the paper around. Invariably by the time it reached Robert, a gruff, red-faced Scotsman, it was streaked with detritus. "This newspaper is absolutely *covered* in honey and margarine" (*mar-jar-EEN*) he'd huff in disgust, peeling apart the sticky pages. He seemed to view himself as the lone adult in a room of 12-year-old boys, their highjinks made even more unbearable by the presence of an indulgent female.

Every so often the person reading the paper would look up to share some disparaging commentary about a politician. "Sauce bottles," Tony remarked. He noted my quizzical look the first time he used the expression. "Sauce bottles," he repeated, launching into an explanation with the kind of long-suffering patience appropriate for a dim-witted American. "You know. Tomato sauce?" (*Tomahto.*)

"Oh! Ketchup!" I answered, still in the dark but ready to be enlightened.

"How do you get the sauce out of the bottle?"

"You turn the bottle upside down and hit it?" I was racking my brain for whatever sexual innuendo he had in mind.

"She's searching for the golden rivet, boys," he said with a wink, then turned back to me.

"No. Say you've got a bottle of Heinz Tomato Sauce, and it's really thick. So thick you can only get it out of the bottle by doing…what?"

"Sticking a knife in to scoop it out?"

He rolled his eyes, then got up and walked over to the fridge, pulling out a bottle of nice cold ketchup, which he handed to me. Setting one booted foot on the chair, he moved into lecture mode.

"Show me how you get the sauce out of the bottle."

Without opening the top, I turned it upside down and shook it rapidly.

"Exactly," he said.

I blushed as it hit me: The politician was a wanker.

"So," I continued, hoping to shift attention away from how easily I'd been suckered. "What's a golden rivet?"

"Ah," said Tony, glad to remain in the spotlight. "Well, let's see. Where shall I begin, men?"

"Start at the beginning!" called George.

"You see, in naval culture, there's this tradition. You tell the new recruit that there's a single golden rivet on the ship: just one in the entire, massive hull. The rest of the rivets, of course, tens of thousands of them, are steel, because gold is expensive, and in any case, it would be useless for riveting since it's so soft. You knew this, right?"

"Um, well, no," I answered. Metal was not my medium. He rolled his eyes.

"You tell the new sailor to go and look for the golden rivet, because when he finds it, there will be a great reward."

He took a sip of tea, pausing for dramatic effect.

"But what really happens is, when he's got his head down a hatch or stuck out a porthole, you pull down his pants and give him one in the backside. Not that I would ever do such a thing, of course."

Robert's gaze was steadfastly glued to the editorial page.

I was the new recruit. Fortunately, I gathered, I had survived my initiation.

2. Dream On

A Thing Worth Making, I: Hunting-Badcocke

WHEN I was 13 my mother let me move home to London from the boarding school where I had spent the previous year and a half. She was in her early 30s then, and living in a tiny flat while she pursued a degree in fine arts. She took to sleeping on a fold-out couch in the 12'-square expanse that served as our common living space and gave me the closet that the real estate listing had called a bedroom.

It seemed I needed remedial instruction in the wake of my time at this particular boarding school, a liberal establishment founded on the belief that children are born knowing everything they will ever need. The point of education, according to this philosophy, is to help a child unfold, rather like a delicate leaf in spring. My leaf was unfolding without yielding the academic development my mother had reason to expect from me, so I was enrolled at a crammer for girls.

The headmistress, Miss Ava Hunting-Badcocke, was a petite woman of around 40. Trim, blond, and always impeccably dressed, she might have made a career as a Burberry model had she been amenable to taking direction. But being ordered about was not Hunting-Badcocke's M.O. Beneath her polished looks and aristocratic bearing stirred the soul of a drill sergeant.

When my mother took me to visit the school just before the start of spring term, we found a tidy row house. "You will arrive by 7:30 each morning," Miss Hunting-Badcocke informed me. "No need to ring the doorbell; just let yourself in."

"You will walk down the hall to the cloakroom, where you will remove your coat and shoes." She ushered us briskly across the checkerboard-tiled floor to an area furnished with a row of hooks and a bench with cubbies below. "This is your storage compartment, Nancy." My name had already been written on the label. "You will keep your ballet slippers here." She pronounced this the English way, with the emphasis on the first syllable: *BAL*-lay.

"You do *have* ballet slippers?" she asked with a raised brow. No, I did not have ballet slippers. Clambering through muddy brooks in old Wellington boots was more my style. My mother assured Miss Hunting-Badcocke that we would buy some before the first day of classes.

"Naturally you will come to school in dresses and skirts only. We do not allow trousers. Each morning you will find your exercise books from the previous day in your storage compartment, where the teachers will leave them for you after they have corrected your work. Retrieve those books and bring them into the front room for inspection."

She trotted back up the hallway to a side door, then passed into what had once been a living room, prior to its transformation into the residential equivalent of an airport security checkpoint. A pair of windows looked out to the street, but the view was screened by layers of net curtains. The far wall was lined with built-in bookshelves on either side of a gas fireplace. In front of the fire lay a feather mattress, at its center a small, snoring pug. "This is *Gaston*," she said, pronouncing his name in French as she gently rearranged his tartan mohair throw, making sure that only his head was exposed. The pug slept through her ministrations.

A prim desk stood next to Gaston's bed, arranged so as to limit the width of the opening into the next room. "You will queue up here," Miss Hunting-Badcocke continued, waving from the front of the house to her desk. "Open your exercise books to your corrected work, then wait until I call your name."

"Once I have inspected your work, you will leave the room in this direction," she gestured toward the narrow opening, turning so that she could squeeze through the space, then leading us through her dining room and out across a courtyard to the classroom building.

By the end of the first week it had become clear that the point of this daily parade was for each of the students to be publicly humiliated. Miss Hunting-Badcocke would glance through our exercise books, reading our scores aloud for all to hear. There was no praise for assignments done well; as she reminded us often, "Excellence is its own reward. Why do anything unless you are going to do it well?" But punt on a fact or misspell a word and "Hunting Bad Cock," as we soon began to call her, turned into a dragon. "Seven out of ten, Amanda? Please tell me that you are not *really* this pathetic. You simply *must* apply yourself."

The pain was magnified by the fact that we were seeing our corrected work for the first time. With only a few minutes between collecting our books and relinquishing them to Miss Hunting-Badcocke, those of us who cared about our performance developed a habit of compulsively checking our scores as soon as we picked up our work, in case we needed to devise some creative explanation for our shortcomings.

For me, Hunting-Badcocke's tactic was potent motivation to study. I did not want to be burned at her stake with the whole village watching. It wasn't long before I'd picked up a handy technique for getting back at my sister when she annoyed me: All I had to do was say "ten out of ten." This became my mantra as we walked home from the bus stop. "Ten out of ten!" I'd chant insufferably. "Ten out of ten!"

Even more damning than the academic corrections were the personal insults. Every so often some overweight girl would find herself trapped in what we called the Straits of Badcocke, wedged between the wall and the sharp outside corner of the headmistress's desk. "Oh, Gabriella," Hunting-Badcocke would sigh, loudly enough for all to hear. "You need to lose twenty pounds. I shouldn't need to rearrange the furniture just so that you can fit into the school." She delivered these indignities with such a striking lack of empathy that I often wondered whether the poor girl's parents had given the headmistress express permission to belittle their daughter in an effort to induce some sort of post-traumatic anorexia.

Since I was doing well academically, Hunting-Badcocke remarked that I needed to up my game in the area of personal appearance. "Nancy, do you possess a hairbrush? If so, please ask your mother to instruct you in its use." If the problem wasn't my hair, it was the wrinkles in my blouse or my sagging knee socks, all such instances of sloppiness supposedly indicative of my low self respect.

Inevitably at some point during each morning's inspection the room would fill with a foul smell when Gaston farted. We rolled our eyes – it only took one experience of Hunting-Badcocke castigating a student who dared comment on this phenomenon to learn we'd better keep quiet – and prayed that the methane would not be ignited by the nearby flames. We joked in secret about how the entire school might disappear in a conflagration sparked by the dog's delicate digestive system. "*Gaston!*" Miss Hunting-Badcocke would cry in feigned surprise as she grabbed the can of air freshener she kept on her desk. "Really, *mon cher*. Try to do better."

But God help the student who neglected to eradicate the noisome evidence of her own trip to the bog. One day Hunting-Badcocke paid an afternoon visit to the classroom building, where someone had obviously just taken a dump. "Everyone in the hallway now!" she commanded like a penal warden, marching from room to room. When we had gathered together, she bellowed "WHO JUST USED THE LAVATORY?" Needless to say, there was no answer. "Well," she went on. "I see that you are all a lot of cowards. There is a reason why I keep the lavatory supplied with plenty of air freshener. It is extremely rude to subject your fellow students and teachers to such a disgusting smell. In the future, USE THE AIR FRESHENER." We did.

The training at this boot camp for adolescent girls circa 1973 was designed to get us up to speed in the subjects that might gain us entry to what Hunting-Badcocke called "good" schools, which is to say private establishments. I'm not sure why my grandparents, who were footing the bill, considered it critical that my sister and I avoid public school at that point in our lives, but it may have had something to do with the time we'd spent in the close company of the hippies who had shared our childhood home in Florida, introducing us to their daily regimen of pot smoking and anti-capitalist values. By the fourth grade I had been attending school stoned. My clearest memories involve the cafeteria, a realm concerned less with nourishment than social display. The highlight of lunch hour was my friend Claudette's Jell-O jiggle, a kind of upright limbo in which she shook a trembling mass of artificially flavored strawberry down her bare arm. We were all happy to donate our dessert to this cause and stood around her cheering, eyes agape. By the end of the year our combined sacrifice had enabled Claudette to master a degree of muscle control and friction modulation that would have made her a shoo-in for a career in pole dancing.

One day while riding my bike to our elementary school in Miami, I was struck as never before by the number of dead squirrels, birds, and raccoons at the edges of the busy street as an endless stream of vehicles rolled past, their drivers oblivious to the carnage wrought by their daily commute. The mangled bodies symbolized an economic system that disrespected nature, even life itself, and school was obviously a training ground for its participants. I wanted no part of it. I turned around, pedaled home, and informed my father that I would not be returning to school. "There are too many dead animals. I can't take it," I told him. He called the principal and told him we were switching to home school.

My father assigned his office assistant, Bambi, to be my teacher. One of our early lessons involved learning to copy maps, an essential life skill if there ever was one. She showed me how to copy an outline using a grid. "Just draw in some squiggles around the edges," she instructed as I worked on a map of Florida's east coast.

"But what about everyone who lives along those bays and beaches?" I asked, concerned that such a *laissez-faire* approach to cartography might result in the flooding of countless homes, drowning the pets who lived in them. (Never mind their human inhabitants, who were of less concern to me in those days.)

"Oh, don't worry about that," she said. "It's just a map."

It wasn't long before we dispensed with this farce and I sought instruction from the young people who were living in assorted small structures they had erected around our tropical half-acre backyard. I learned to make whole wheat bread, tofu and carrot pizza, and home-churned ice milk, washed my clothes in a puddle, and took cold showers to fortify my character. I dispensed with my hair brush and allowed my dirty-blond tresses to spin themselves into a head of dreadlocks that unsophisticated acquaintances of my parents dismissed as filthy matted hair. In a nod toward formal study, I read several entries in the *World Book Encyclopedia* each day and was so taken with the one for panpipes that I wrote to the editor and asked for plans that I might use to make a set. I signed my letter *Norman Stanley Hippietoe*, an androgynous persona I had invented to replace my birth name and gender. I was elated when a letter addressed to Mr. N. Hippietoe arrived in the mail, even though it carried the disappointing news that the publisher could offer no plans for constructing the instrument.

Meanwhile, my sister lamented her diminished quality of life ever since our parents had banned junk food and shopping at the mall. Taking matters into her own hands, she stole a bundle of cash from the vending cart used by one of our resident hippies who sold nuts and dried fruit to stoners at the local park. "Where did you get those?" I asked when she showed up with a new pair of clogs and a jumbo bag of Jolly Ranchers. "I found twenty-five dollars on the sidewalk outside school!" she exclaimed, thrilled by this blessed stroke of fate. Her cover was blown when Rob, the park vendor, discovered his money missing. My sister went to live with our grandparents, who indulged her with the pleasures of a typical middle-class American childhood circa 1970.

So I imagine the rationale behind private school had something to do with our proven susceptibility to influences our grandparents deemed dangerous. Private school at least offered the prospect of closer surveillance. And goodness knows we had some catching up to do when it came to academic work. So despite the daily insult of Hunting-Badcocke's inspection, I soaked up the structure like a desiccated sponge plunged into warm water.

In addition to the basics – Latin, art history, math, and English grammar – the curriculum at Hunting-Badcocke's school emphasized writing skills, with essays on topics ranging from "Compare and contrast the paintings of Monet and Manet" to more abstract assignments. Most memorable to me was the pair of apparently contradictory sayings "A thing worth doing is worth doing well" and "A thing worth doing is worth doing badly." I found the second incomprehensible and wrote the sort of confidently superior diatribe you might expect from a 13-year-old for whom nuance is an alien concept. Why would a teacher assign such a silly topic when Hunting-Badcocke herself was constantly reminding us that there was no point doing anything unless you were going to do it to the best possible standard?

It would take decades for me to grasp the meaning of this second saying. But grasp it I eventually did.

A Thing Worth Making, II: Hotel California

IN THE 20 years after my tyrannization by Miss Hunting-Badcocke I attended high school in London, went to college and dropped out, trained to make furniture, and began my career as a cabinetmaker.

I launched my last serious attempt at escape in 1990. While running a custom-furniture business with my second husband in a rural area near Bloomington, Indiana, I began taking classes part-time at Indiana University, eager for some intellectual stimulation. As I sat in the lecture hall the first day contemplating the room's hundred-plus capacity and contrasting it with my experience at Cambridge, where my Hebrew class had seven students and the Aramaic class had one – me – I was gripped by an urge to flee; I have never felt at home in crowds. But as soon as the professor launched into his lecture on religion, medicine, and suffering, I was hooked.[1] The classes were a revelation, so broad in their subject matter and so relevant to contemporary life that I decided almost immediately to pursue a new, more fulfilling, and more secure career: teaching at the university level.[2]

An academic adviser urged me to apply for a scholarship, which covered the cost of tuition. I sought every possible grant, teaching internship, and essay contest along the way, which paid for books. Taking classes year 'round, I worked half-time in our business, meeting with prospective

---

[1] The professor was Robert Orsi, now Professor of Religious Studies and History and Grace Craddock Nagle Chair in Catholic Studies at Northwestern University. My enthusiasm for the subject matter was genuine.

[2] Note to all adjuncts and itinerant professors: I know.

clients, dealing with design work and bookkeeping, as well as helping my husband with deliveries and installation. I left the marriage during my first semester of graduate school; we were divorced soon after. I lived on fellowships and assistant instructorships supplemented with freelance design work for another furniture maker in town.

But by the time I completed my master's degree in 1995, it was clear I was not cut out for the life of publish or perish. What I'd wanted to do was *teach*. A master's in religious studies, without further training in the School of Education, would not qualify me to teach in public high school, and there was no private school within 50 miles that might hire me. I didn't want to move. So teaching was out.

I moved into a 1920s bungalow across the street from a homeless shelter and started applying for jobs. With a degree in hand, I imagined it would be easier to find work that would bring me into contact with people instead of mute material, which I'd consistently found depressing in my woodworking career up to that time. Over the next four months I sent out employment applications while taking any odd jobs I could get. It was a trying year for the would-be employed in south-central Indiana; listings in the "Help Wanted" section of the local paper included such enticements as "LOOKING FOR A CAREER WITH CHALLENGE? Parkland Pork Enterprises is seeking a Production Manager to oversee all aspects of pork production!" and "TRAIN TO BE A CHILDREN'S ETIQUETTE CONSULTANT: You will join over 600 consultants who are providing the highest quality programs in the United States and abroad."

I had a couple of interviews for office work but still had not been hired when I was called to interview for a clerical position in one of the university's academic departments. The pay was low, but the university offered some of the best working conditions in town. I would spend my days in one of the historic campus buildings, a limestone Tudor originally constructed as a dorm. I could already see myself walking the mile and a half to work each morning, the perfect distance for a pedestrian commute, and eating my lunch of leftovers on the lawn at the center of the quadrangle. I was certainly qualified for the position. All I had to do was show my interest and enthusiasm, which were sincere. I dressed in a nice skirt and blouse and walked to campus feeling confident that *this* job might well be mine.

When I arrived at the office, the administrative secretary took me into a meeting room and introduced me to the chair, Professor Jameson, who was seated at the head of the table. Standing up, he shook my hand and smiled warmly. "I just had to meet you after reading your résumé," he began. Things were looking good.

"We're not going to hire you," he continued. "You're seriously overqualified. But I called you here so that I could ask you in person: Why would such a talented and accomplished person apply for a clerical job?"

How dare he waste my time just to satisfy his curiosity? After four months of job hunting, I needed some income. To hell with Professor Jameson. In fact, to hell with all of those people who'd turned down my applications. I was going back to what I knew. And I had a lead on a job.

"Hello, Andrew? This is Nancy Hiller. I'm one of the students who rented your house while you were in the Middle East."

A renowned Egyptologist, Andrew had recently spent two years in Cairo researching death and taxes circa 2500 BCE. It was during his second year away that I'd left my marriage and moved into town. The listing for his place in the "Shared Housing" section of the classifieds had opened with the word "Beautiful." A sucker for beauty in buildings and gardens, I'd immediately scheduled a visit and ended up renting a bedroom for the year, sharing the house with a six-foot Amazon named Sadie who was an MFA student in painting, and her dog, Raquel.

The house was a single-story brick bungalow built in the 1940s. The kitchen and bathroom were still largely in their original state, and while the kitchen functioned adequately, the bathroom was a disaster. The top layer of sheet vinyl, which had been applied over several previous strata, was so worn that some creative soul had plastered it with contact paper in a black-and-white checkerboard pattern to suggest something classy. The deception was almost convincing. A small vanity constructed of crumbling particleboard was propped up with a 2x4 to keep it from collapse. The recessed medicine cabinet was pitted with rust, and the tub, sink, and stool were all shell pink, a color that at the time was still not old enough to be considered campy.

None of the renters during Andrew's two-year sojourn abroad had met the homeowner. We knew only that the place belonged to a faculty member, so we referred to our landlord as The Professor. Our personal contact was a real estate agent, Bonita, who managed the property. Whenever Bonita was scheduled to stop by, Sadie would hide Raquel in her car, because the lease strictly forbade pets. Our hazy image of The Professor made it easy for Sadie to take other liberties as well, such as removing the fancy tasseled curtains from the living room windows to use as tablecloths for dinner parties with her art school friends. In the aftermath of one of these I inquired about the red wine stains on the otherwise pristine fabric. "The Professor left the curtains in the house," Sadie explained. "What did he expect?"

To make up for Raquel's long days stuck inside, Sadie ended each evening with a vigorous game of field hockey in the living room. Just as I turned off my bedside light, their match would start. *Thwack!* went the hockey stick as it scraped the hardwood floor, launching a tennis ball over to the fireplace or couch. The scratch of scrambling dog claws would follow as Sadie returned the ball and begged for more. *Thwack!* Scratch scratch scratch. *Thwack!* Scratch scratch scratch. Every so often this cheery rhythm was interrupted by "*SHIT!*" followed by Sadie's clogs clomping across the bare floor as she fetched a dustpan and brush to clear up a shattered glass or vase. Coupled with my anxiety over having left my marriage, this nightly routine left me with a sleep disorder that took years to abate.

"You know that bathroom in your house?" I continued, on the phone to Andrew. There was just the one bath, though someone had installed a second toilet in the basement, presumably for emergencies. My question was obviously rhetorical, a way to ease my way out onto a limb that I suspected was unlikely to bear my weight. "It desperately needs some work. I've never done any serious remodeling, but I'd like to start, and I would remodel your bathroom for just twelve dollars an hour plus materials at cost in exchange for the opportunity to learn."

"That's an interesting proposal," Andrew replied. "Come by next Tuesday and we'll talk."

"I can't believe I just did that," I exclaimed to my boyfriend, a professor of microbiology, as soon as I put down the receiver. It was so brazen – an act of sheer desperation, in fact, which accounted for my ability to pull it off.

Andrew hired me to remodel his bathroom after seeing my furniture portfolio. Nine months later, his bathroom was finished.

I loved the variety of the work – carpentry, tile, painting, and plumbing – and my conversations with Andrew about design and related topics, such as his first colonoscopy and which drug store offered the best deals on Johnnie Walker. Working as a design-build remodeler just might provide the relative autonomy and contact with people I'd longed for when making furniture and cabinetry for anonymous customers. I loved old houses and thought I could turn them into my market niche.

    I set up a bare-bones workshop in my basement, furnishing it with a few bits of equipment purchased with my VISA card at the local building supplies store. I bought business insurance in case of calamity. And after Andrew broke his ankle cleaning his gutters, an injury that called for more regular assistance from Johnnie and left him scooting down the basement stairs on his backside to use the house's single working toilet, I added a basic medical policy as well. I found a beat-up F-150 with a radio that only picked up AM stations and became a regular listener to a call-in show hosted by a therapist who shared Hunting-Badcocke's confidence in the character-building potential of verbal abuse. I began to get referrals for bathrooms, bookcases, and built-ins that ranged from recessed medicine cabinets to entire walls.

    Dark, damp, and accessible only via a set of rough limestone steps that made delivering large objects a challenge fit for a skilled contortionist, my shop set-up was pitifully inadequate, and some of my work fell short of professional standards. Of course I can't pin the blame entirely on my shop; it's a poor craftsman who blames his or her tools, etc., etc. My attitude played a huge part. I considered my work a stop-gap, something I was doing to support myself until I figured out what I should really be doing with my life – preferably something in an office, where I would use my mind and spend my days engaging with fellow human beings. My customers didn't mind the imperfections in the work; they were just happy to have their space improved. By the time I was finished, a once-blank wall in a bungalow's hallway had a recessed linen cupboard, its doors, trim, hardware, and finish indistinguishable from the original 1920s woodwork around it. The addition at the back of a Tudor Revival cottage with cigarette holes in the Berber carpet and generic 1980s trim around the windows and doors now sported a well-laid oak floor, built-in bookshelves, and woodwork to match the original part of the house.

    It wasn't long before I switched from general remodeling back to the custom furniture and cabinet work that had comprised the first 10 years of my career, focusing on period-style work for old houses. With this change came a creeping return of the perfectionism I'd cultivated during my City & Guilds training. "Is this good enough?" I'd asked Mr. Williams in those days, handing him my latest effort at a dovetail or miter. In his soft Welsh accent he always threw the question back at me: "Do *you* consider it good enough? If you need to ask the question, you most likely know the answer." As I scrutinized the joint, he'd invoke some woodworking hero's aphorism and apply it to the matter at hand: "Do you intend this chair to hold up to daily use so that its owner can pass it down to his grandchildren?" (In those days, all references to hypothetical persons involved masculine pronouns.) "Always remember: There's no point doing anything unless you're going to do it well." With that kind of responsibility, "good enough" could always be better. So I kept trying. Five hours to cut the dovetails for a drawer? No sweat. Perfection was an end in itself, and time was not an issue.

But as a professional running an enterprise on which my livelihood depended, I soon realized I'd have to adapt my way of doing things according to what my customers were willing to pay. Excellence might be its own reward, but striving to achieve it throughout every commission was going to bankrupt me, given the actual market for my work, especially since I was living alone, with no potential support from a second income. I found myself in effect giving away hundreds of dollars' worth of work on each job while attempting to satisfy my internalized Mr. Williams – and the dollars I was writing off were on top of whatever part of the overage I asked my customers to cover.

If you have a well-employed spouse, or perhaps a parent or other benefactor who's willing to subsidize your admirable refusal to compromise, you might not be acquainted with the sense of dread that grows with each passing week an invoice goes unpaid. In my first such experience, I was contemplating a second cash advance on my credit card when I mustered the guts to call my client.

"Hello, Rob? I was wondering whether you received the bill I sent for the balance due on your sideboard." This was the built-in sideboard that had started with a budget based on a plywood carcase joined with biscuits and screws – a sound, efficient technique I'd learned at a high-end custom office furnishings shop in Vermont, which would let me put furniture-quality materials and care into the visible parts of the cabinet – before my internalized Mr. Williams began ripping apart my plan. In those days, Mr. Williams usually won. So I built the case in solid oak using hand-cut dovetails, with integral drawer runners and a frame-and-panel back. I carefully pointed out the first-quality craftsmanship and materials to my clients at the end of the job, hoping that their appreciation would justify the additional cost.

"We got your invoice," Rob replied. "And we ain't payin' it." A high-school teacher of English and social studies, Rob did not routinely abuse his native tongue. I got the message: They were outraged by my charges.

"Um," I replied, my voice beginning to crack as I contemplated the looming due date for the next month's mortgage. "Could you at least pay the balance of the original estimate?"

"Well of course, Nancy. You know we love you and your work. But when Josie saw your bill, she said 'Nancy didn't build this cabinet for us. She built it for herself.' Honey, you can masturbate to your heart's content on your own time, but you shouldn't expect your customers to pay you for it."

It was a painful but important lesson.

A Thing Worth Making, III:
Human Factors Engineering

LAST SPRING I went through our house picking out clothes, books, and furniture to pass on to my niece. Along with an early 20th-century schoolmaster's desk, the library of classic volumes our parents bought when my sister and I were kids, and some clothing that no longer fit me was a set of four storage cubes I'd had since the late 1970s. I bought them from a branch of Habitat, the iconic store launched by British designer Terence Conran, who pursued the ideal of making practical, clean-lined furniture affordable to all. The cubes are made of 1/2"-thick particleboard with pine veneer and appear to be sprayed with clear lacquer in a satin finish. They were sold in flat packs for home assembly with screws – no joints or glue involved. In other words, they are just the sort of stuff you'd never expect to last.

But I'd had these storage cubes just shy of four decades. Despite 16 moves, one of them across the Atlantic, followed by others that involved traveling between states as far apart as Vermont and Montana and being carted up and down innumerable staircases, they still looked good and worked as well as when I first assembled them. The secret to their longevity? I simply treated them well, using them as they were intended to be used: for storage, not as ladders or to prop up the car when changing a tire. Barring the failure of the glue that holds together the particleboard itself, they should last at least as long again.

I drove my truckload of offerings down to Florida the next time I visited my family. At the time, my sister and her daughter, who was 13, were living in a two-story cottage behind my parents' house.

"We've been invited to a small dinner party at the home of an English furniture maker," my mother told me as we began the wretched task of unloading the truck on a 98° day with 100 percent humidity. I was resigned to hauling the stuff up the long flight of rickety stairs. My mother thought the prospect of a dinner party would brighten my mood.

"Gavin Pratt is his name," she said as we lifted the heavy desk. "He's highly acclaimed. He started out in sculpture. That's how we met, at art school in Hammersmith." We put the desk down on the landing and took a breather. "It's a bizarre coincidence that we both ended up living in central Florida," she continued. "His reputation as a furniture maker today is positively stratospheric."

Once we'd settled the desk in my niece's room, my mother went next door to make some tea, while I lugged the 23 boxes of family books up the stairs. I'd read fewer than a dozen of them, and that was back when I was being "home-schooled," at the age of 11. Although the books survived the hippie years – unlike so many of our possessions, which were given away as examples of consumerist excess – they bore the scars of that grand era when my parents eschewed such bourgeois comforts as air conditioning. Concerned about hazardous chemicals, they had also cancelled the pest control service, thereby making our old house in south Florida an ideal habitat for bugs. Cockroaches were especially fond of the books' cloth binding. *The Decline and Fall of the Roman Empire: Volume Three* had crumbled almost as tragically as the embossed gold pillars depicted on its spine. The warp of *Moby Dick*'s linen cover hung in tatters, leaving patches of bare cardboard where the roaches had consumed the weft. Poor old *Uncle Remus* had turned white with mildew, and silverfish corpses had been pressed like dried flowers into *Sister Carrie*'s pages. Some people might have thrown them away, but I can't throw out a book – never mind *these* books: handsome editions, produced to be heirlooms. Sinclair Lewis's *Main Street* was embellished with drawings by Grant Wood; *The Brothers Karamazov* featured lithographs of villains, dandies, and distraught family members weeping on cobbled Moscow streets. These were treasures that deserved to be handed down to the next generation. I was relieved to be passing them on to my niece.

Once I'd unloaded the last box of books, only the pine-veneered storage cubes remained. They cowered at the back of the truck like a row of illegal immigrants who'd just been busted. But instead of being terrorized by an officer from Immigration and Customs Enforcement, the cubes were attacked by my mother. "You've got to be kidding," she declared, casting me a withering look. "You drove this particleboard junk all the way down here? What's a cabinetmaker even doing with this kind of crap?"

"I bought those things in London before I did my training," I whined.

"They were my first-ever furniture splurge, back when I had no money, so they have sentimental value. Besides, they're practical. And Wyatt will get a kick out of their 1970s aesthetic."

Everything about Gavin said "designer," from the tangerine-orange khakis, vintage Madras plaid shirt, and Keds to the silver ponytail and meticulously curated two-day stubble, which added a manly edge. "Hey there, Mary Lee, welcome," he said in an English accent somewhere between that of a BBC announcer and a fishmonger from London's East End. The more I heard him speak, the more his accent called to mind a radio that resists being firmly tuned to a single channel. "Come and have a drink."

Turning to me, he shook my hand. "A fellow woodworker, I gather from your mum. No doubt you'd like to see my studio."

"Well, actually," I thought, "what I'd really like to do is get *myself* a drink after an afternoon of toting the proverbial bales." But before I had a chance to voice this thought he was directing me toward the door. "Righty ho. Let's pay a quick visit to the studio, then."

It was twilight as we made our way across the lawn to a large cinder-block building behind his house. "Hold this a mo, luv."

"Don't call me 'luv,'" I thought, chafing at his apparent assumption that I would warm to this Brit expression of familiarity. He handed me his martini glass while he unlocked the door.

It was a spacious shop, well lit and outfitted with a tidy mix of old and new equipment. "I'm working on a dining table and chairs for a client in Miami," he told me. "Quite a famous bloke, actually. To tell the truth, he's got such a big name that I'm not allowed to say it. Not that that's anything out of the ordinary in my world. These days it's rare for me to work for anyone who's not routinely written up in *Esquire* or *Vanity Fair*, that sort of thing."

"Which part of London are you from?" I asked, curious as to the origin of his accent.

Ignoring my question, he turned his head to the right, saying "Come an' take a look at this table and chairs" as he strode toward his workbench. The dining set was inspired by the work of French Art Deco designer Émile-Jacques Ruhlmann. The table, made of rosewood, was stunning. A cross between Deco and neoclassical, it had an extending top that could seat an intimate foursome or expand to accommodate 10. It was waiting to be finished, as soon as the chairs were ready.

"Double tenons hidden in those miters around the seat," he remarked.

"Ever use those darlin's? I'm telling you, they are *quite* the challenge to pull off. But what a sturdy bit of join'ry they are. Those chairs will last forever. On the other hand, so will everything I make. That's one of the reasons my clients are willing to wait years for an opening in my schedule."

"I took a look at your website," he went on. "Nice enough work, but really…. 'Period-authentic furniture and built-ins?' It's all been done before, 'ain't it? You couldn't *pay* me to do that type of guff for common punters. On the other 'and, someone's got to do it, so I daresay it might as well be you."

Now that he'd established I didn't even rank high enough to engage in a pissing match (not that I am ever inclined to take part in such bullshit) I thought he might answer my question. "Which part of London are you from?" I asked again.

"To tell you the truth, luv, I'm not from London at all. Actually, I'll let you in on a secret. I'm not even from England." It seemed the vodka had loosened his lips. "I'm from a tiny burg in rural Missouri, a dump no one's ever even 'eard of. Now this is top secret information I'm sharing with you, 'K? I don't mind telling you, as we obviously don't travel in the same circles. Well, that's the understatement of the millennium, innit?!" he chuckled at his little joke. "Still, not a word to anyone. Hush-hush."

He grabbed a can of roasted nuts from his workbench, pulled off the top, and tossed a handful into his mouth. "'Em'r good," he said with a wink, his voice suddenly an octave deeper, his drawl thick as tar.

"I never knew my daddy," he continued in his native accent, apparently relieved at the rare chance to let down his guard. "Grew up with my grandparents. Pap was a machinist, but woodworking was his hobby. He taught me a lot." He tossed another handful of nuts in his mouth. "All I ever wanted to do was get out of that shit hole of hog farms and speed. Am I ever glad I did. Today the area's drowning in meth labs. Don't get me wrong. I'm grateful to my grandparents for raising me, but Jee-zus. I wanted to make something of myself. You hear me?"

"I had a talent for drama and art in high school, which got me a scholarship to art school in London," he said, reverting to his English accent, now firmly tuned to the BBC channel. I imagined it must feel risky to stay out of character for very long; he might forget who he was. "That's where I met your mum all those years ago. And quite a fox she was, I tell you. Always had an eye for the older ladies, I have."

"Well, what's with the English accent?" I'd spent 16 years in England, starting at a much younger and more impressionable age than he had, but whatever accent I'd absorbed had begun to fade as soon as I stepped off the plane on my return to the States.

"Three years was more than enough for me to master an accent. Drama, remember?"

"So, Gavin… What kind of parents in rural Missouri name their baby 'Gavin Pratt'?" I asked, suspecting that in this case, as Mr. Williams would say, I knew the answer already.

"Well obviously I changed me name," he replied with the merest hint of defensiveness, which seemed to bring out the fishmonger in him.

"And what was your given name?"

"No one needs to know. It was a common name. It's meaningless now. The only thing that matters is that today I am Gavin Pratt. 'Gavin,'" he said, striking a pose found in portraits of 17th-century European aristocrats. "Is there a more quintessentially English name? And if I do say so myself, I make an excellent 'Pratt.'"

I muffled an uncontrollable snort, attempting to disguise it as a half-formed sneeze. Apparently, while three years had given dear Gavin enough time to craft a pretentious persona that would be convincing to most Americans, it had not been enough for this particular bit of English slang to enter his vocabulary. He was in effect telling the world that he was an excellent pussy.

"So that scholarship to London got me more than a degree in fine arts," he continued, blissfully unaware of the irony I was now savoring. "It also provided a key that magically unlocks the checkbooks of the rich and famous. Seriously, do you know a single American who doesn't fawn over any and everything U.K.?"

Well, I knew at least two – myself and my friend Alex, whose own experience of English boarding school had provided valuable insight into some of England's less admirable traits, the persistence of class distinctions and the arrogance toward former "Colonials" among them. But Gavin was clearly not interested in having his monologue interrupted by such details. "I mean, forget *Downton Abbey*; that blond bird on the telly's sellin' millions' worth of loo rolls by encouraging Americans to talk about their bums! I'm tellin' you, if it's British, you Yanks just eat it up. So once I'd perfected my persona, I'd've been a fool to let it go," he said with a grin.

"Well then, enough of this rubbish. Let's get back to my guests."

As Gavin directed us to the table I noticed that the chairs he was currently building in his shop were exactly the same design as those we'd be using for dinner. "Cool," I thought. It's always interesting to see whether a chair that handsome is also a pleasure to sit in. Chairs are a special subset of furniture making; it's challenging to come up with a design that not only looks good, but also seats a range of body types comfortably. I took my seat. The chair was as comfortable as it was good looking.

Across from my mother and me sat Gavin's next-door neighbors to the west, Sybil and Monica. Sybil was a professor of history and gender studies at the town's private liberal arts college; her wife, Monica, was executive director of a non-profit arts organization. To my right sat Tristan and Jenny, a couple of recently married hipsters. Tristan ran an organic composting operation that collected restaurant waste, turning it into black gold for the gardening program operated by the local food bank; Jenny was a partner in the town's first small-batch coffee roastery. As Gavin informed us, Tristan's mother, an actress whose face appeared frequently on magazine covers, had commissioned him to build "the kids" a bed.

Rounding out the table were Persis and Earl, Gavin's longest-term clients; in fact, they had been his very first clients when he started his business upon moving (of course they did not know he was moving *back*) to the States. So even though they were not particularly wealthy and were certainly not famous, Gavin continued to accept the occasional commission from them. Persis, a slender blond in an amber silk sheath, had spent her best years as a stay-at-home mom. Earl was her opposite: a portly Southern attorney with a bowtie and ruddy complexion. His curly light-brown hair was cropped short and remained damp with perspiration throughout the evening.

Before long it was clear that Earl was challenged by social situations. No matter who was speaking, Earl would break in, blurting out his opinion. Small-batch coffee roasting? "Frankly, I've never understood what's not to like about Folger's," he exclaimed. "It got me through law school at Harvard. Do you really need more than that? This is what's wrong with our country today: People think they're too good for the basics. Everything's becoming unbearably precious." Crippling funding cuts for Monica's organization? "If people want to 'make art'" – he held his right index finger to his open mouth, suggesting an urge to vomit – "let them persuade bona fide customers that what they're doing is worth paying for. I for one am sick to death of being taxed to support ass-humping milquetoasts."

In an attempt to restrain herself from getting involved in the increasingly tense conversation, my mother helped Gavin clear the table. While they were out of the room, Tristan decided to have some fun baiting Earl on the subject of politics.

"Can you *believe* Mitch McConnell, claiming that the Constitution requires the next SCOTUS nomination to be made after the end of Obama's term?! What kind of fools does he take the American people for? Why, anyone who reads English can see the Constitution mandates the 'president' to make that nomination: the one who is presiding – present tense. It doesn't say that he or she 'may' make that nomination. It doesn't say that he or she 'should' make that nomination. It says that he or she 'shall' nominate the next Supreme Court justice."

"Goddamn bleeding heart leftists," Earl thundered. "Our country's gone far enough down a road marked 'Hell' with that African Muslim in the White House. Worst president in the history of the United States, bar none." He patted his dripping face with his napkin.

Gavin returned with a tray of crème brûlée to find Tristan beaming in puerile glee. Earl, on the other hand, was crimson: a coronary waiting to happen. Every other face at the table had turned gray with dread. Persis placed a soothing hand on her husband's arm and whispered "*Earl, honey, please calm down*," giving him an imploring look.

Gavin passed around the ramekins, shakily remarking "Well, then. Let's have our 'afters.' Have I mentioned how truly lovely it is to have my friends gathered around my self-made table for a cordial evening?" He sat down and smoothed his napkin across his lap.

Unfortunately Tristan would have none of this peacemaking. He was on a roll; pushing Earl's buttons was too much fun. "Oh, say, Monica, did I hear you're having an exhibition of work by transgender artists next month?" I sensed that this was a topic *guaranteed* to make Earl want to vomit. But Earl managed to hold himself impressively in check.

"Well in fact we are," Monica replied, choking down her first bite of dessert. "One of our board members suggested it as a way to enlarge our demographic. We see it as an exciting opportunity for a diverse swath of the community to come together in a festive atmosphere while learning about the importance of trans culture."

"And they've contracted with Swallow Spirits as well!" Sybil added. Swallow Spirits was a new craft distillery, its name a clever play on words: simultaneously an imperative to act – "Swallow spirits (preferably ours)!" – and a beloved species of birdlife. "Swallow will be serving signature cocktails crafted with botanicals nurtured on the new green roof of the county jail. It's a ground-breaking program designed to get inmates involved in productive activities they can parlay into employment opportunities upon their release."

"Productive activities?!" Earl exploded. "Since when is growing watercress or basil to flavor the kind of ridiculously pretentious drinks you're describing a 'productive' way to earn one's living? Truly, I fear for this country. We have become a nation of pussies."

Now I was starting to feel sorry for Earl. However successful Tristan's mother had been in Hollywood, she'd clearly failed when it came to teaching her child manners. Tristan was a spoiled brat who either had zero sense of social propriety or, as I suspected, was accustomed to being indulged…which, in the end, was largely what Earl found so objectionable at the national level.

"Well hey, old man, if we're gonna be a nation of pussies at least we should do it to the best of our ability," said Tristan. He raised his glass. "To excellent pussies and no half asses!"

Earl started to say something, but Persis hushed him. Like a pressure cooker on the boil, he began tapping his foot and mopping his brow. She stared at him sternly. He kept his mouth shut, I'll give him that. But the pressure was clearly too great. Unable to sit still, he began rocking back and forth in his chair.

I know what happens when large people rock in dining chairs. I leapt to my feet and had opened my mouth, but before I could get the words out, there was an ear-splitting CRACK as the chair's joints gave way and Earl fell flat on the carpeted floor.

I Used to Do What You Do

"HOW MUCH time do you spend in the shop, and how much in writing?" asked a friend of a friend who'd waved me over to sit with him at a holiday party. He'd noticed my bio in the list of contributors to an area magazine and knew I'd written a couple of books.

"I pretty much write in my spare time," I said. "Mainly on weekends, if work in the shop doesn't require my presence there. The books in effect pay nothing. The magazines at least pay something, but it's not enough to cover my overhead and operating expenses, let alone live on."

When I really cranked out articles for the local magazine where this acquaintance had seen my bio, I could make about $15 an hour. But this calculus relates to net income, not the gross revenue required to maintain a business – and certainly not my cabinetmaking business. It doesn't matter whether I'm writing, sleeping, or working billable hours; a host of fixed and related expenses still have to be paid.

"Oh, please," he said dismissively. "What kind of overhead and operating expenses do you have? You work from home and have no employees."

I was taken aback. Why did he think he knew anything about my business? We scarcely knew each other. Did he think I was posturing as a professional while secretly just "crafting" in my garage?

"You know," he added, rolling his eyes. "I used to do what you do." He'd mentioned once that he had worked briefly as a carpenter during what he called his hippie youth; as part of this personal exploration he'd tried his hand at cabinetmaking before concluding that, while he loved the work itself, doing it for a living involved more tedium and less creative freedom than he could bear. Some years later he got a job as assistant art director at a major magazine and worked his way up to a well-paid position, from which he had recently retired. He pushed his chair back from the table and walked away without giving me a chance to respond.

"Tosser," I said under my breath as he sought out someone else to use as a sounding board for his oversized ego. Then again, I realized, I had no idea how I would have responded had he stayed. If he really was that ignorant of the costs involved in operating a microenterprise – aboveboard, mind you, not under the table – a meaningful, non-defensive response would take some time for me to articulate, not to mention a willingness on his part to listen.

I grabbed his unused napkin and pulled a pen out of my bag. The numbers were fresh in my head; I'd spent the previous weekend going through the year's accounts to get a jump on tax preparation.

"Overhead and operating expenses, 2014," I wrote at the top of the napkin. That pompous jerk was not going to get away so easily. Between bites of salad I listed the categories I could remember, adding a few explanatory notes:

- "Business insurance (coverage of shop building and contents, liability, goods in transit, etc.)
- Equipment rental (e.g., trailers for delivering large jobs)
- Health insurance. (Many people whose health insurance premiums are subsidized by their employer have NO CLUE what it costs. Mine is $506 a month for so-called "wellness coverage," i.e. I have to pay for almost everything out of pocket, and with a $6,000 deductible. My husband and I are both self-employed, so we each pay through the nose.)
- Permits (e.g., for parking in our highly regulated city)
- Accountant's fees
- Mileage

At this point I realized I had lapsed into completely irrational behavior. He would never read such a list, not to mention the parenthetical notes, which were likely to grow in length now that I was getting warmed up. But perhaps the sheer number of items listed would at least impress on him that I run a business with real-world operating expenses. So I continued writing.

- Packing & shipping
- Website-related expenses
- Office supplies & printing
- Subscriptions to trade publications
- Disposal of non-recyclable, non-compostable shop & jobsite

     waste
- Phone & internet at shop
- Dues to professional organizations
- Shop utilities (electricity & water; the insurance industry now pretty much refuses to cover woodworking shops that are heated by means of a woodstove, and there is no way I'm going to run a business like this one without insurance)
- Repair & maintenance of equipment; replacement blades, cutters, etc.
- Bank charges (e.g., the cost of checks) for business account
- Business travel expenses; I do sometimes teach, speak, & deliver furniture out of state. (These are not vacations, like those publishing-world boondoggles you brag about at cocktail parties. They are bona fide working trips.)
- Business tangible property tax
- Professional photography for the portfolio, when I can afford it
- Taxes related to payroll: state unemployment tax, Medicare & Social Security matching taxes, etc. Years ago, my accountant advised me to organize my business as a Subchapter-S corporation instead of continuing as a self-employed proprietor."

My hand was cramping, so I put down the pen and took a sip of cabernet. The cheese board at this bash was always a vision of abundance. I added a wedge of crumbly aged cheddar and some crackers to my plate – along with the wine, a perfect combination. By this time I had completely covered the napkin on both sides, but I sensed that I was far from finished. Grabbing a couple more napkins from the buffet, I got back to work.

"All of the above (and more) must be covered before I pay myself a penny. And this is not including investment in new tools, machinery, etc., which amounts to thousands of dollars. In 2014 the above expenses came to just over $20,000. I don't know…maybe that's chump change to you. Not to me.

"And yes, my shop is behind my house. But I no longer live in the house. I had to move out during the recession, which absolutely gutted my business. During the worst year, my *gross sales* (i.e., *including materials*) were $17,000. I slashed the overhead and everything else to the bone. I relied on my credit card to pay lots of bills, a debt that took the following two years to pay off. I'm incredibly lucky that my boyfriend at the time – now my husband – invited me to move in with him; at least that way I no longer had to pay for all my living expenses on one decimated income.

"That year from hell, I obviously could not even pay myself minimum wage after covering the overheads. You're probably wondering why I didn't just go out and get a couple of jobs – you know, bagging groceries, cleaning toilets at the office supply store. (BTW, there were none of those jobs available. Because recession.) Believe me, I thought about it. One friend, a nationally recognized furniture artisan, confided that he was seriously contemplating a job flipping burgers because he wasn't getting orders. Another put his business in a holding pattern and relied on his wife to support him (he was lucky she could). But I calculated that doing spec pieces and writing would be a worthwhile investment in future business opportunities, even if I had to rely on my credit card to make that investment. Thank God my bet paid off.

"I have been renting my house out to cover the mortgage & property taxes. You probably think this means I have Even. More. Income. But no. Renting the house increased the monthly payment because I no longer qualified for the homestead tax exemption. Also, insurance rates for a rented property are quite a bit higher than for one that's owner-occupied. So the income from rent just *barely* covers the monthly payment. But at least I still have my shop, for which I am profoundly grateful.

"Don't get me wrong. I could, in fact, make more money if I only worked in the shop seven days a week and didn't do the writing. But going back and forth between these kinds of work is critical to my sanity.

"All of which is to say that yes, I do have overheads and operating expenses."

I folded the napkins in half, put them in my pocket, and made my way through the crowded room over to the dessert table. I was balancing a slice of chocolate hazelnut torte on a cake knife when I spotted him spooning tiramisu seductively into the mouth of a woman who looked young enough to be his daughter. I stood there holding the torte on the knife while she closed her lips around the spoon and shut her eyes with an expression of orgasmic delight. Once she had recovered I walked over and tapped him on the shoulder. "Rafi," I said, pulling the napkins out of my pocket, "I have something for you." I unfolded them and laid them on the table in front of him.

"OK," he said distractedly as he scooped up another spoonful for his friend, who seemed to be incapable of feeding herself even though she was old enough to drink wine. "Thanks."

I happened to pass their table on my way out a half-hour later. The napkins were just where I'd placed them, but crumpled now, the ink smudged into a dark blue blur. Seeing me roll my eyes, a man at the next table said, "I don't know what was written on those napkins, but it sure must have been funny. The guy sitting there was reading it to his daughter – or was she his girlfriend? – and at one point she laughed so hard she spat out a mouthful of pudding. Geez, what a sticky mess."

The Excellent Craftsman

IT WAS a weeknight in the summer of 1997 when I got the call. The voice on the line was gravelly, with what seemed like an urgent tone.

"Nancy? David Larimer here. Wondering whether you'd do me the honor of allowing me to take you out for dinner. I'm thinking of moving to Bloomington and have to find a shop. You always know what's going on there. Will you meet me tomorrow?"

"Hmm," I thought. This was odd. I had been acquainted with David several years earlier through the regional woodworking scene. He and his wife lived in a rural part of a neighboring state where the rolling landscape, affordable property, and remoteness from zoning authorities had drawn a number of artists.

At the restaurant downtown he sought out a table for two in a dark corner. "What's good here?" he asked. "You always know what's good."

His deference to my purported sophistication had me puzzled. Since when was I an authority on restaurant menus, let alone real estate? As a single woman supporting myself on whatever commissions I could get, I struggled to pay my mortgage. I was certainly no real estate insider, monitoring local listings.

Once we'd ordered, he explained the reason for his invitation. "Laura and I are getting divorced. Splitting up the house, land, everything. We should net around $300,000."

"Oh, wow," I responded. "I'm sorry."

"How about I move in with you?" he said with a wink and a boyish grin, putting his hand on my arm.

"So funny," I answered dryly. It took some effort to focus on the outlandishness of the idea and not allow its appeal, at least as a fantasy, to color my response. He had an animal physicality and intensity about him that I'd always found powerfully seductive.

"Anyway," I went on, doing my best to be businesslike, "my shop is in a tiny garage." This was the garage of the house next door. I had recently moved out of my basement up to grade. Having a window was a luxury that I would never again take for granted. "The place has no insulation. It's freezing in winter and hot as hell in summer, aside from which it's on property that's zoned residential. Any disgruntled neighbor could shut me down in a second."

He moved closer. "I don't need a lot of space. Just a little corner for my bench and some tools."

His persistence threw me off guard. This whole dinner was beginning to seem a little crazy, but I couldn't help feeling flattered. I'd been divorced – twice, by then – each time on good terms that had allowed both parties to move on with our lives even while we worked out our split. So I could relate to David's readiness to go forward with his own plans at this stage in his marital schism.

And I had to admit I was intrigued. I'd seen an Italian modernist-style chair of David's in a woodworking magazine. Even though that kind of modern stuff did nothing for me aesthetically back then, it was an astonishing piece of craftsmanship, and I wondered what had prompted this man whom I knew primarily as a rural carpenter and cabinetmaker to create an object of such refinement. I wanted to get to know him better.

Just as compelling was his unrestrained interest in me. Every man in my life had been diffident at best. As a high school student in London I was never asked out by English men – well, at least men my own age. A well-known TV personality once stopped me on the street when I was 16 and asked if I'd like to go for a drink. "Gross," I wanted to say, but in those days I would never have caused intentional offense, so I simply replied "No, thank you" and carried on down the sidewalk, my cheeks flushed with shame – on his behalf, not mine, as I was pretty sure I'd read somewhere that he was married. The only men close to my age who were willing to approach me were from Mediterranean countries who'd come to London for a university education. I was so socially clueless that I was flattered by any invitation and felt obligated to say yes, even to a stranger on the street. Of course I should have known that these encounters, based on nothing more than my appearance as an athletic girl in her teens, were destined to lead to one-night stands. For the next 20 years I had invariably been the one to do the pursuing. No man had ever seemed fully confident of his attraction to me or ready to express it. Until now.

As we said goodbye he squeezed my hand. "I'll call you next week," he said with a rascally smile.

"Nancy? David Larimer here. I'm in town and wonder if I can stop by and whisk you out to my little farm in Putnam County."

It was late afternoon and I was in the middle of drilling 1,600 shelf support holes for a set of built-in book shelves destined for a client's home library, so the impromptu invitation a few days after our dinner was easy to accept, even if it meant losing a couple of paid hours.

He picked me up in his diesel truck and we headed south on the highway. "Here, have one of these," he said, pulling a couple of Boddington's ales out of the compartment between the front seats, open container law be damned.

On the two-hour drive he talked about his work. "Going into modernist furniture was the smartest thing I've ever done," he began. "There's so much money in the northeast. People have taste and the wealth to satisfy it – not like around here." He flicked his right hand as though he'd accidentally picked up a turd, a gesture of disdain I would come to recognize, since he used it so often. "No matter what I charge, I can't keep up with orders."

When we arrived, he took me to his shop, where he was working on a rosewood sideboard commissioned by a client in Connecticut. I'd seen this kind of sideboard in a book about contemporary furniture that I once received as a gift; it was more like a piece of functional artwork than anything most people would call furniture. Clean-lined, with sculpted legs and drawer pulls, it was one of the most technically and aesthetically impressive pieces I had ever encountered. Seeing it in the making, I suddenly had a different perspective on the entire style.

"Look over here," he called, pulling open the top three drawers in one section of the case and pointing to a set of dovetails he'd recently finished cutting by hand. They were a study in delicacy and perfection.

"Come see this," he whispered with a conspiratorial smile, putting his arm around me and leading me over to his workbench, where a three-part display-case joint, apparently an exercise, was hanging from a hook. He pulled it down and took the joint apart, then handed it to me to put back together. It was like a puzzle. The fit was flawless.

"How on earth do you know how to do this stuff?" I asked. "Pshaw, it's simple," he answered. Really. You have no idea. You could do any of this – probably better than I can."

"Just give me a minute, dear." He headed toward a doorway that led into another work space. "Laura asked me to cover up her prints to keep the fly droppings off them. This business of taking care of her work in addition to my own is getting old." He flicked his hand.

"So she still works here?" I asked. "Yes, until we get things sorted out, she continues to work in this studio. Just grab that corner, will you?" he asked, shaking out a sheet of wadded plastic sheeting. He pulled his end tight and fastened it to a wooden shelf with a couple of spring clamps, then came over to where I was standing and pressed his hip against mine as he clamped the plastic. I felt myself blush.

He turned to me with a wide smile. "Enough about work. Let's get out of here."

As we walked up the hill to the house he pulled me down on the grass, where we sat and talked a while. The view was breathtaking, with forested hills that went on for miles.

Abruptly he broke into my reverie. "Take these off," he said with a grin, tugging playfully at my jeans.

The speed and passion of the romance felt like a dream come true. It was electrifying to be so wanted. I hadn't felt that alive in years. A couple of days later he called in the late afternoon. "I have to see you," he said in that now-familiar urgent tone. "Can I come over?"

He pushed me against the wall and kissed me as soon as I opened the door. "You're intoxicating," he breathed. "I can't stop thinking about you."

Sex was only a small part of the attraction, at least for me. David was by far the most excellent craftsman I had ever known. I was awed by his artistry and passion for his work. The same well-worn fingers that sawed those crisp joints and pared those fluid forms were now caressing my naked body. As we lay in bed, he invariably spoke about his latest commission: a coffee table, a mantel clock, a set of stacking chairs in bent laminated oak. His craftsmanship went well beyond work with wood, tools, and finishes; he was also a published scholar. He made regular trips to major libraries and galleries to research original mid-century works and the craftsmen who had made them. He pored over the sort of details that most people wouldn't even notice, in an effort to master each craftsman's language. His obsession with his work set him apart from anyone I had ever known and made me swoon.

I'd hear from him once every week or so, always on the spur of the moment. I became as attuned to the rattle of his truck's engine as one of Pavlov's dogs to the ring of the bell. The smell of diesel exhaust became an aphrodisiac.

One evening, feeling particularly happy, I decided to call him and say good night. There was no answer. A few minutes later the phone beside my bed rang. "You can't call me here," he whispered. "Laura's here tonight. I'll explain next time I see you."

What the hell? Were they sleeping together? Perhaps this was a fluke. I realized that I had allowed myself to be so swept up in the romance that for all I knew, they might have been sleeping together all along.

"I don't know what's going on with her," he told me a few days later as we sat together on my worn 1940s couch. "Anita, our baby, grew up and left for medical school. Laura wants to be with her baby. She's spending most of her time in the city, living with Anita. Maybe it's menopause. She's also decided she doesn't want to be a printmaker any more. She wants to work in advertising sales for the regional newspaper group. For months now she's been taking classes and buying new clothes. So many pairs of shoes and handbags…." He flicked his hand. "Ridiculous."

Laura was working in ad sales for the company that published my daily paper? I recalled his pretext for inviting me to that first dinner. Surely she could have just handed him the real estate section.

I realized with chilling clarity that I had been demoted from True Love to The Other Woman. I had never wanted that role, in this or any other relationship. But by now I was in so deep that I found the thought of not seeing him unbearable.

I tried to rationalize my quandary with helpful advice from friends. "Nancy, you're not the one who's doing something wrong," Sam told me. "David is. He's the one who's married." Sometimes I just surrendered myself to being in the moment without judgment, hoping that one of these days he would make up his mind and leave his marriage.

One day I was describing the relationship to another friend. "I was in that kind of relationship once," she told me. "It was a few years after my divorce. I was head over heels in love with the man. He kept saying he was going to leave his wife for me, but he never did. I broke it off a couple of times – once for an entire year. But I kept going back. It went on for eleven years until one day I forced myself to acknowledge that he was never going to leave. Men in those situations don't leave. They just don't. You need to break things off if you want to be in an honest relationship."

Eleven years? To hell with that. I finally knew what I had to do.

The next time we were together I told him it was the last time. I couldn't do it anymore.

"Damn it, dear," he said with a tragic air. "We're like Yuri and Lara in *Doctor Zhivago*; we were made for each other, but we can't be together." This abdication of responsibility for a situation clearly of his own making was so preposterous that for a few seconds I found him pathetic. Sadly, that sense of emotional liberation evaporated quickly. Breaking up with him was one of the hardest things I'd ever done.

The next evening I rented the film of *Doctor Zhivago* out of morbid curiosity. The casting of First World War-era Russia through a 1960s Hollywood lens made me cringe. Still, later that winter, when I spotted a balalaika in a customer's library it brought tears to my eyes.

I waited hopefully for spring's daffodils to break through the snow. Maybe by then he would be free, and we could be together. Sure, it was sappy, but my heart was broken.

Spring brought no call. I told myself to be patient: Things would get easier by the day. Slowly I got over him. I found an affordable shop on a buffalo farm outside of town and moved my business there. I was seeing a new man. Three years had gone by when, one day in early spring, the phone rang. "Nancy, it's David. David Larimer. Laura and I have broken up. Can I come see you?"

My heart leapt. At last, the call I'd hoped for!

"Come see me at my new shop," I urged, pushing the reality of my new relationship to the back of my mind, at least for a couple of hours.

I showed him around. The shop had no running water. But the space was large, the location idyllic. I was working alone in the countryside and no longer cared about not having a toilet, though the previous winter's deep snow had given me a new appreciation of what it means to freeze one's ass. I took him out to sit in the warmth of the sun on the chilly afternoon.

"So, what's been going on?" I asked.

A look of chagrin came over his face. "Well," he paused. "Nothing's changed, actually. God damn it, I just had to see you."

Five more years came and went. We'd bump into each other every so often. I was polite but had finally convinced myself that despite his many fine attributes, he was deluded when it came to love. I had moved to another location, my first serious shop of my own, and was building my furniture and cabinetmaking business in earnest. I had also recently started dating a man I adored.

One day I got a call. "Nancy? David Larimer here. Can I come see you?"

By this time I knew better than to let my heart swell. I couldn't believe his lack of shame. But it was always good to hear about his latest work.

Half an hour later, there he was in person, at my shop door. I told Daniel, my employee, that I'd be back in a few minutes and took David to the house. We sat down on the old couch, which I'd recently had reupholstered. He took my hands in his and looked me in the eye. "Come live with me in London."

"Are you actually living in London now?" I asked matter-of-factly.

"Well, no, but I could be. Come with me! We could make such beautiful music together." He was like a little boy, drunk on fantasy.

Obviously it was ridiculous, yet even so, after eight years, I felt that tug. London? With David? The possibilities were tantalizing.

I told my closest friend, a scholar of medieval English literature with an open mind and her own history of interpersonal escapades that would raise some eyebrows. "Oh Nancy," she commented dryly, "this sounds just like the kind of desperately romantic thing Bernard would have proposed." Bernard, the cheating former husband who was by then on his seventh wife while maintaining a clandestine affair on the other side of the Atlantic.

The next time he called I told him – gently, mind you – to cut the romantic crap. "David, you are a world-class bullshitter. We can be friends, OK? I would like that. I love hearing about your work. It's such an inspiration. My partner's 10-year-old son would be fascinated by your shop. I know it's a ridiculously long drive, but how about if Mark and I come over one day with Jonas so that we can all get to know each other like actual *friends*?"

"Well," said David in a surprised yet agreeable tone. "That would be grand! We'll do a cookout. I'll get some brats. Thursday evening, OK?"

On Thursday afternoon, an hour before we were due to set out on the two-hour drive, David called. "Damn it, Nancy, I'm sorry, but I'm not going to be able to do our cookout."

In the background I thought I heard a woman's voice say "Put the dime in the parking meter, David. I want you *now*."

Shortly after this I was visiting an acquaintance who happened to be an old friend of David's. Rudi was aware that I knew David professionally but had no idea of our intimate history.

"He's done it again," said Rudi, looking up from his computer, where he was checking email, with an ironic smile.

"Who?" I asked. "Done what?"

"David Larimer. Got himself entangled with a woman – this time a good friend of mine – only to let her down."

"Who's your friend?" I asked, my curiosity piqued.

"Patti Reynolds. He had her thoroughly convinced that he and Laura had broken up and he was ready to move in with her. When she couldn't reach him by phone one evening she got suspicious and drove all the way – across state lines! – to their house. There was the whole family: David and Laura, their daughter Anita and her husband, the grandkid, sitting around the table for a big meal, just like a Norman Rockwell painting. When Laura answered the door, Patti wished she could march right over to David and bitch-slap him in front of everyone."

A few years later I attended a day-long finishing workshop in a nearby town. The workshop had been sponsored by a regional woodworking club, most of its members men in their 50s and 60s who were passionate about their hobby and regarded the craftsmen who appeared regularly in national magazines with adulation. By this time I'd had a few articles of my own published in those magazines; the organizer of the day's event had mentioned that he'd seen my work and was glad to have me there.

By the end of the afternoon, the workshop presenter had me convinced that I should invest in a particular type of brush he recommended for shellac. Conveniently, he had several with him for sale.

Rifling through my bag, I discovered that I hadn't brought enough cash. He wasn't set up to accept credit cards. "Just send me a check," he said, handing me his business card.

"Are you sure?" I asked. "I mean, of course you can count on me to send the check. But not everyone would be so trusting."

Overhearing us, the workshop organizer stepped between the presenter and me. "Nancy, you can always trust an excellent craftsperson. Anyone who's that scrupulous about his or her work is going to have the ethics to match."

No.

IT'S AMAZING how unaware most people are of what's involved in running a business that makes things, especially if that business involves the design and building of custom commissions, as opposed to mass- or even limited-production manufacture.

For starters, many people imagine that a business owner's time is her own, to work or not, as the whim may strike. Their place of work keeps going when they're off sick or on vacation, so they take for granted that yours does, too. Take Martin Luther King Jr. Day off to volunteer for your neighborhood's creek clean up and people assume your business is paying you for that time, just as their employer is paying them for theirs, or that you can at least write off the loss on your tax return. "That's not the way it works," I've tried to tell them. "In taking this day off, I am giving more than my time and effort to haul VCRs, mattresses, and tires out of the creek; I am giving an entire day's gross revenue – not just my personal pay, but the portion of my overhead that my labor today would otherwise have covered." But try to explain this to most people and their eyes glaze over.

Start your own business and you'll find yourself hit up regularly for donations to schools and nonprofits. "That Arts and Crafts wall shelf you did for *Fine Woodworking* would make a handsome contribution to our auction," read an email several years ago from an acquaintance who was on the board of a local organization. "And if you wanted to throw in a copy of your latest book, that would add a warm personal touch." Never mind that I had $1,200 worth of labor and materials invested in the wall shelf, or that, as author of the book, my discount was just 40 percent off the cover price, meaning that I would have to spend $18.95 plus tax and shipping to buy the copy he was inviting me to give away. "Your donation will bring you invaluable exposure to just the kind of clientele you seek," his message continued: "people who have a household income of at least $100,000 per annum: pillars of the community who are active in civic affairs."

"OK," I've thought on occasion. "It's a good cause. I'll make this donation." But do so a few times, only to learn that your work was purchased for not much more than you paid for the materials alone, and it gets old. "What? They bought that thing for just two hundred dollars?" I asked my acquaintance when he called with what he thought would be joyful news.

"Well, what did you expect?" he replied. "No one goes to an auction expecting to pay full price. Auctions are all about getting a bargain. Tom and Sylvia know your work and love it. That's why they made sure that theirs was the highest bid. They told me they were overjoyed at the prospect of getting their own Nancy Hiller. 'And such a steal!' Sylvia said. You should feel honored."

"But I thought the whole idea was to raise money for your organization. I would have expected these pillars of the community to pay the full price for any item in the auction, maybe even more, knowing that their donation was going to such a worthy cause."

"What exactly will I be supporting?" I asked on another occasion. Another friend, another request for a donation, this time made by phone.

"You'll be helping us meet our overhead expenses and pay our executive director," she replied.

"Didn't I just read that your executive director makes $42,000 a year?"

"That's right," she said, her voice swelling with pride. "We were thrilled to be able to raise Matthew's salary to a living wage a few years back. After all, we consider it important that our executive director be paid enough that he doesn't need to avail himself of the services our organization provides."

Now, I'll be the first to agree that $42,000 was hardly a prince's salary in 2013, when this interaction took place. Still, it's far more than I was ever paid when I worked for other people – and more than I have been able to pay myself in most of my years of self-employment. My parents raised me to shoulder a reasonable[1] weight of noblesse oblige, and I recognize that my life is blessed in countless ways. So in principle I have no problem entertaining the idea that in such cases I am being asked to contribute indirectly to the salary of someone who makes more than I do. I think?

---

[1] OK, perhaps unreasonable

Then there are the people who ask if I will hire them as an apprentice because they want to learn to do what I do. "I'm sorry, but I'm not in a position to take anyone on at present," I usually say.

"Well, how about if I just come and watch you work so that I can learn?" a few have responded.

"I'm sorry, but I can't let you do that," I reply. "Simply having another person around a woodworking shop is a distraction, which is dangerous, in addition to decreasing productivity. Never mind the fact that you're not just going to absorb skills by osmosis; I would have to take time away from my work to show you how to do each step of every process."

"Here's how it works," I want to continue, but usually restrain myself. "If you want me to teach you, you need to pay me. Why would you imagine that woodworking is any different from other skills that you would learn at a school where you pay to attend classes?" It's not that I'm a greed-head. There are serious expenses involved in running a shop, not to mention the small matter of my need to actually earn a living.

"But I can't afford to pay," some of them go on. "And you have a business." *What does that even mean*, I wonder? Does it not occur to these people that my business, as modest as it is, has taken decades to build? My shop did not just fall out of the sky into my backyard. Nor does owning the means of production guarantee that I will continue being blessed with paying work. Keeping those orders coming in is itself a part-time job for most of us. No. "Having a business" is at least as much about bearing a daunting degree of responsibility to my customers, various branches of the government, and the fellow tradespersons I occasionally employ as about getting paid to do work that I find meaningful.

I once received an email message from someone who wanted to get into professional furniture making. He had a master's in philosophy – or maybe it was anthropology or religious studies; I can't remember – and had taken some woodworking classes. He was moving to Philadelphia to pursue a doctorate. "My plan is to become a professor for my day job and be a furniture maker in my spare time," he wrote. "Do you have any advice about how I should run my business?"

"Ask your favorite professor what he or she does in his or her spare time," I replied, aware that most of my academic friends, especially those engaged in the Herculean task of getting tenure, routinely work well into the wee hours and laugh ruefully at casual questions about dating or hobbies, never mind running a business on the side.

For many years I considered it my obligation to do what I could for others who wanted to get into the trade. A few people had been generous with me in the early days, so I wanted to pay it forward. I would agree to spend a few minutes, which, as often as not, turned into an hour. Meet them for coffee or breakfast downtown. Give them a glimpse into the realities of my world, which I knew were very similar to those of my cabinetmaker friends. Help a young person get started – even, sometimes, give a few paid hours of IRS-approved casual employment to someone who needed them.

I once got a call from an acquaintance who worked at a homeless shelter for women. "We were hoping you'd hire one of our clients," she said.

"I'm sorry," I replied. "I am not in a position to hire someone right now." I mentioned the tax and insurance costs associated with hiring an employee. I spared her my thoughts on why hiring someone with no experience simply because she was a fellow female would have been absurd.

"Well, would you hire her under the table?" she responded.

"No," I replied, this being the one word I could summon forth in my near-speechless state.

Had this representative of a social service organization that accepts government funds and is bound by stringent regulations really thought this through before asking me to engage in a blatantly illegal practice that could put my own livelihood at risk? I mean, things would have been different had we been in Nazi Germany and she'd been asking me to hide a family in my cellar or attic. But this was Indiana in the 1990s. She and her client had options.

After dozens of these calls and emails over the years, I recently explained to a caller who said she wanted to apprentice in a woman's shop – only a woman's shop would do, she insisted – that I could not take her on as an apprentice. "Well can I come and talk about other opportunities to learn more about woodworking?" she asked. I had to say no, explaining that I was under the gun with several deadlines. "Well can I just come and SEE your shop, then?" she asked. I hated to be unhelpful, but I really needed to get back to work. And even though I know from experience that you can't get anywhere without being persistent, I was finding her refusal to hear what I was telling her increasingly exasperating. "I'm sorry, but no," I said, aware that my bluntness might well come back to haunt me. (Bloomington is a small town.) I suggested she try calling a pair of women furniture makers who I imagined might well be in a position to take her on as an apprentice. She hung up on me.

Family: Mary Lee, Magda, and Herb circa 1967. Photo by Richard F. Busch (rfbphotos.com)

With the base of a Welsh dresser, my first commission, in 1980. The cabinet was built of pine from a lumberyard in Wisbech. The photo was taken in the front yard of our cottage in Friday Bridge; the Chequers Pub is visible in the background. Fred and Gladys's fish & chip shop was a couple of blocks away.

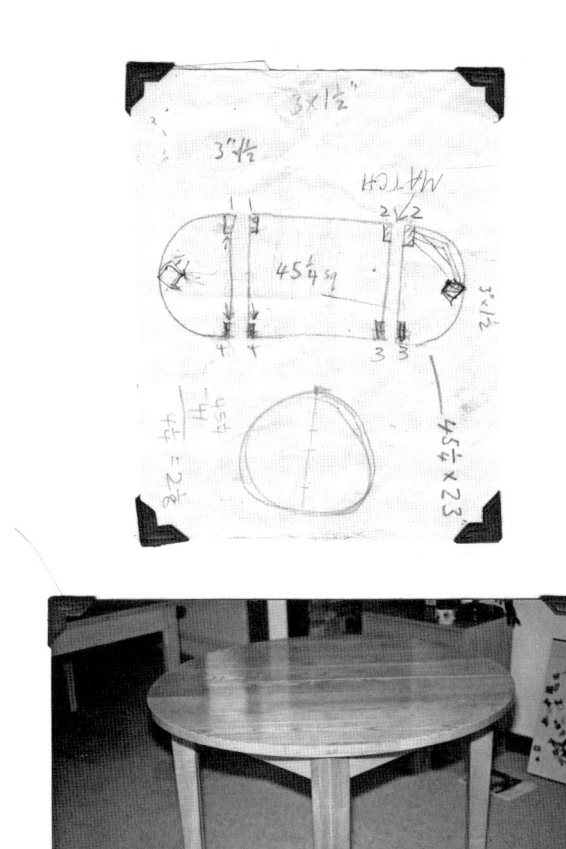

The drawing my employers at "Farmstead Furniture" gave me to build a dining table in ash, circa 1986. The table was made in three parts: a central square section with two half-round sections that could either be added to the ends of the square part or attached to each other to create a circular table, as shown here. In addition to the tops, the legs had to join up so that when sections were put together, each leg would be a tapered square in section, instead of a tapered rectangle.

Bathroom remodel, 1995-96. I gutted the room to the studs and rebuilt it using porcelain mosaic floor tile, ceramic wall tile with a pomegranate frieze, a new pedestal sink and faucet, and recessed medicine cabinet made in my basement workshop. I subcontracted the refinishing of the tub, which changed the color from pink to white. Photo by Kendall Reeves, Spectrum Studio of Photography & Design (spectrumstudioinc.com)

1997. Photo by Kendall Reeves, Spectrum Studio of Photography & Design (spectrumstudioinc.com)

82

Top: Kitchen cabinetry in Shaker furniture style. Cherry cabinets with hard maple counters, made in my basement workshop circa 1997.

Right: Detail of drawer cabinet in the Shaker-style kitchen. Photo by Kendall Reeves, Spectrum Studio of Photography & Design (spectrum studioinc.com)

Dancing Tables, circa 1999. Curly birch, mahogany, and ebonized poplar. A commission made in my garage workshop. Photo by Kendall Reeves, Spectrum Studio of Photography & Design (spectrumstudioinc.com)

Edwardian Hallstand, 2002. A spec piece in curly white oak, made in my workshop on a buffalo farm. The piece was later published in *Fine Woodworking*. Photo by Kendall Reeves, Spectrum Studio of Photography & Design (spectrumstudioinc.com)

85

Butler's pantry cabinets for a late-Victorian house, built circa 2003. Quartersawn white oak with reproduction hardware. Photo by Kendall Reeves, Spectrum Studio of Photography & Design (spectrumstudioinc.com)

Daniel O'Grady, who worked with me from 2005-2007, celebrating his Volvo's 200,000th mile in front of Hinkle's Hamburgers on Bloomington's west side.

English Arts & Crafts style sideboard, 2007. Plainsawn red oak. A reproduction of a circa-1903 sideboard manufactured by Harris Lebus of Tottenham. Art glass by Anne Ryan Miller (anneryanmillerglassstudio.com), hardware by Adam Nahas (cyclops-studios.com). Photo by Kendall Reeves, Spectrum Studio of Photography & Design (spectrumstudioinc.com)

Vanity and medicine cabinet in quartersawn white oak and mahogany, respectively, with salvaged hardware. The medicine cabinet has a carved tulip frieze; its doors have additional mirrors on their inside faces for optimal viewing of the back of one's head. Photo by Kendall Reeves, Spectrum Studio of Photography & Design (spectrumstudioinc.com)

Corona Plumosa, 2012. Funded by an Indiana University ArtsWeek grant. Burly silver maple, quartersawn white oak, and black walnut. The piece is a riff on the gaudy Spanish Colonial Revival furniture produced by Showers Brothers of Bloomington, Indiana, in the 1930s and sold nationwide through the Sears & Roebuck catalog. It was selected by Wendy Maruyama for inclusion in the Indiana State Museum's "Fearless Furniture" exhibition in 2013-14. Photo by Kendall Reeves, Spectrum Studio of Furniture & Design (spectrumstudioinc.com)

Coffee table, 2014. Quartersawn oak with swing-out trays and inlaid bumblebees on side and back panels. The hinges are salvaged; decorative strap hardware was fabricated by Adam Nahas of Cyclops Studios (cyclops-studios.com). Photo by Kendall Reeves, Spectrum Studio of Photography & Design(spectrumstudioinc.com)

My husband, Mark Longacre, at the Assateague Island National Seashore, 2016. Photo by John Holmes and Kim Fischer.

Family, 2016. My parents got back together in 1993, after some 20 years apart.

3. Making Things Work

Cat and Mouse

THEY SAY you never forget where you were when you heard the news. President Kennedy's assassination? Standing by the pass-through between our dining room and kitchen. I was four; my mother was in tears. The same applies to 9/11. I had just begun designing a kitchen for a Second Empire-style mansion in a small town on the Ohio River. With its mansard roof fringed in decorative iron spikes and brooding cedars at the front entrance, the place had an intriguingly foreign aspect, as though it might have been spirited off a barren mountaintop in Transylvania to its new home in the Midwest.

This architectural gem was one in a row of imposing houses on a hill that rose sharply from a street overlooking the river. Each house had a set of stone steps leading up the slope to the front door, leaving no doubt that its occupants dwelled in an elevated realm. A gravel path concealed by shrubbery led off to one side, where it terminated in a tradesman's entrance. A century ago, dairy, coal, and ice deliveries would have reached this entrance from the back alley, but by today's standards the narrow alley is barely passable, virtually guaranteeing that your vehicle will be gouged or have the passenger-side mirror mangled. So most service providers park on the street and approach from the front.

One morning I got a call from a contractor who was working on a proposal to remodel this house's kitchen. We'd met at an historic preservation conference. Now he needed some help with design in order to get an accurate sense of the scope of work.

We shook hands on the street and chatted as we walked up the path. As soon as he rang the doorbell a chorus of barks and wails erupted inside. The door opened, revealing a petite woman with long blonde hair – 35, I'd say, stylishly dressed in black Capri pants with a clingy white top and bare feet.

"Hello," she said, addressing Robert as she unlocked the outer door.

"You must be Robert. I'm Fiona."

"And this is Nancy," he nodded in my direction.

Five dogs of indeterminate breeds surrounded us as we stepped inside. "My protectors," she said, shooing them off. "Out with you! On the porch!"

She led us to the kitchen and began describing the job. "I'd like to remove this wall between the kitchen and dining room, and I know I want to get a new fridge and professional stove. Beyond that, I really have no specific thoughts. I'm ready to be impressed." Obviously she was interested in expert help – a good sign. Until we had a plan, there was nothing for Robert to bid on. So I submitted a design proposal the next day, hoping to move things along for everyone's sake. She hired me right away.

She'd mentioned that the house's original cabinets were stored in the basement. Always fascinated by original built-ins, I asked to see them during our first design meeting. "Do you think we could put them back?" she asked. "Well, we could," I told her, "but there are some drawbacks. The shelves are fixed, not adjustable, which will limit your flexibility in storing things of varying height. They're also probably covered in lead-based paint, which will be labor-intensive to strip before we apply fresh paint."

"On second thought, then, let's go with new cabinets," she decided.

I took detailed measurements of the original cabinets and based my drawings on them, making modifications as necessary to accommodate new appliances and the wall that would be removed. Most design professionals switched to computer drafting years ago. I still draw with a pencil and rule. When it comes to basic drafting, computer programs strike me as overrated. The investment in buying the software and learning to use it is costly, primarily in time – and as with all things electronic, programs are updated regularly, often requiring new investments in software and equipment. I am still not convinced that the promised benefits would be worth the expense for my business. Although design and drawing are essential parts of my work, they take up very little of my time; the overwhelming majority goes into building and installation. My drawings are simple and efficient; they convey the basics – form, dimensions, mechanical specifications – and I augment them with samples of wood, finishes, and hardware.

After meeting with Fiona to discuss the preliminary drawings, I left them for her to show her husband, Bradley. Ordinarily I make a point of meeting with both spouses in a married household to make sure we're all on the same page. Having both parties present helps avoid misunderstandings, not to mention the occasional attempt by one spouse to subvert the other's preferences. Fiona had assured me repeatedly that her husband was too busy to meet. A well-known attorney with a firm in a nearby city, he was willing to leave the meetings and management of the kitchen remodel to her.

A couple of days later she was ready to meet again.

"We really like your ideas," Fiona said as she ushered me into the butler's pantry. "But Brad's worried about the drawings."

"Worried?" I asked.

"He doesn't like the idea of paying $65 an hour for drawings done by hand when the entire drafting for our previous house was done in two hours by a guy with a computer. He doesn't see why drawing a kitchen should take longer than it took to design a whole house."

I explained that my proposal for the design work went well beyond drawings. It involved research into the original kitchen's layout, historically informed interpretation of period nuance, knowledge of contemporary appliances and building materials, and the ability to translate these, along with Fiona's preferences for storage and workspace, into a room that would function practically in 21st-century terms. This wasn't something you could just plug into a drafting program.

"I'll be happy to discuss this with Bradley if that will help," I told her, sensing that she felt trapped between us, a position I didn't envy. If he was that concerned about efficiency and costs, we'd have no problem finding common ground. I had a friend who'd interned at Bradley's firm, so I was familiar with how things were run there. Enormous sums were spent on advertising. No expense was spared in keeping the offices too warm during winter and too cold in summer. The partners had even installed a heated sidewalk leading from the parking lot to the front door, to head off at the pass any opportunistic winter injury claims. Meanwhile, I kept my shop thermostat set no higher than 55° all winter, except when I was applying finishes, and did my drafting at the kitchen table. I made peanuts compared to anyone at Bradley's firm, even the lower-level office staff. If anyone knew how to squeeze a nickel, it was I.

"He's just too busy," she assured me. So Fiona and I continued on our own.

We were close to finalizing the drawings when I received a curt email from Fiona directing me to send a bill for the work I had completed and to hold off on further design pending discussions with her husband.

"Also, please submit a proposal to build the cabinets," she wrote. The next day I dropped off a set of the unfinished plans with a proposal to finalize the design work and build the portion of the cabinetry based on the existing plans.

"Nancy!" she wrote the following day. "Thanks for dropping off the plans. They're great! And the contract. It's great!

"But we have a problem. The drawings aren't complete! How can we make a decision without the completed drawings?"

I picked up the phone and dialed her number. "Hello, Fiona? It's Nancy Hiller. Hey, I just got your message about the drawings. I'll be glad to finish them, but you said you wanted to terminate the design contract and asked me to send what I had finished to date."

"That's right," she said. "Bradley and I think we've paid you enough to cover a set of kitchen drawings and we don't want to pay any more."

"Our agreement is based on charges by the hour," I explained. "I gave you an estimate based on how many hours I thought the work would take, given the scope of work we discussed initially. We still aren't even close to the estimated charges in my proposal, so are you sure there's a problem?" My contract could not have been simpler. Her husband was a lawyer. What was behind this change of plan?

"But we can't make a decision without the drawings!" she cried.

"I'll be happy to meet with you again and complete the drawings in whatever way you would like," I suggested, feeling trapped in a vortex of circular reasoning, "but I'll have to get you another contract to sign. At this point I'm no longer under contract. I'm running a business, and I can't afford to do more design work without knowing that I will be paid."

That night I got an email from the elusive Brad.

> Nancy:
>
> Fiona says that you owe us a sketch showing the final section of work you propose for our kitchen. We expect to see that tomorrow.
>
> Thank you.
> Bradley Billingsworth

This was odd behavior. I had not encountered anything like it in my years of running a business. Still, to placate them, I replied that I'd do a simple sketch showing the further revisions Fiona had asked about. I dropped it off the next day at no charge.

That was the last I heard from them. I followed up by phone a week later, leaving a message, but got no reply. About a month later I called again; this time I left a friendly message saying that I imagined they had hired someone else to do the work, I hoped the project was going well and was sure it would turn out beautifully.

After this I let the matter go.

The following summer I was delivering some furniture to a customer in Florida. As I pulled out of a parking lot in rural Alabama my phone rang. "Nancy," said a woman's voice. "This is Fiona Billingsworth. Do you remember me?"

"Bradley and I were wondering if you'd be willing to talk with us about doing some new design work. I hope I haven't burned any bridges! We've spoken to several other people, but I haven't found anyone I get along with as well as you."

I needed work but was wary of entering into a new arrangement with Fiona and her husband. On the other hand, their house was exceptional. The prospect of creating cabinetry based on the design of the original kitchen made me salivate, and I knew of no one else in the area who possessed the knowledge of kitchen history and the aesthetic restraint to do it well.

"Sure, I'd love to discuss it with you," I replied.

After shooing the dog pack onto the back porch so that we could have our next meeting, Fiona told me that she now had a part-time job. She handed me her card.

Fiona Billingsworth
Customer Satisfaction Specialist

I put it in the Billingsworth job folder. They had hired a carpenter named Dwayne to demolish the kitchen's 1970s iteration. Gone was the acoustic tile ceiling, so out of place in this turn-of-the-century context. Gone, too, the bulkheads, the "Colonial"-style cabinets, the harvest gold laminate counters. The plaster ceiling was still intact, the scars of the kitchen's original cabinetry exposed. The layout had been just as I had pictured it based on the cabinets in the basement. In the northern light of late summer, the room felt relieved. It was beautiful in its bareness.

"Are you going to have Dwayne do the rest of the job?" I asked, wondering who was going to be the general contractor. Robert's name had not come up since that first meeting. "No," she replied. "He keeps going walkabout. I ask him to complete the work, he shows up, spends a few hours, and leaves. He doesn't return my calls. He claims he doesn't know what I want him to do with the kitchen. And he's working on other jobs while he does ours. When I put my foot down and told him we need him to finish, he yelled at me."

"Wow," I replied. "That's certainly no way to treat a customer. I can't imagine how he stays in business with that sort of behavior."

A few days later when I drove over to confirm some measurements, Bradley was just leaving for work. Fiona introduced us. Bradley seemed quite a bit older than his wife – late 50s, maybe.

"We told Dwayne not to bother coming back," Bradley remarked. Fiona must have mentioned my inquiry about their now-former contractor. "He hasn't even billed us for the work he's done to date. And now we're not sure we want to pay him. I hope he has a contract that will hold up."

I was confused. Was Bradley actually concerned for Dwayne, or was he trying to convince me that he was a sympathetic fellow, while actually planning to deny his carpenter payment? If the former, why bother mentioning the solidity of his contract? Why not just pay him?

"That's not our only problem," Fiona continued after giving her husband a sweet kiss goodbye. "We're suing our plumber. He sabotaged our water line – cut it on purpose! We had to spend $200 to get it repaired. He was mad at us. His contract said he would put in new toilets, but when he billed us he wanted us to pay him for removing the old ones. I mean, how could you even put new ones in without removing the old ones? What does he think we are – idiots willing to pay more than we agreed to? On top of that, when I told him we were taking him to court, he said (here she affected a whiny tone) 'Fiona, I am dying of cancer. I don't want to go through that.' As though we would fall for that kind of bleeding-heart crap."

Whatever problems they'd had with other contractors, they were going to need someone to run the job. Rebuilding their kitchen to the professional standard they obviously expected would require expertise beyond my own. There was electrical, plumbing, plaster, and tile work. The hood Fiona had ordered for over the stove would require external venting, so a large hole would have to be cut in the brick wall at the rear of the house – not something I wanted to be in charge of. She also wanted custom storms for the kitchen windows.

I asked her about Robert, the contractor who'd brought me over the first time, but she said she was disinclined to call him. So I referred her to a friend who is an expert in historic preservation. He in turn suggested that she hire Rick, a contractor who also happens to be a friend of mine, to oversee the rest of the job.

"I don't know that I want to get involved with these people, darlin'," Rick said that night when I called to discuss the job. "It sounds like there have already been a few red flags."

"I know," I replied. "But they were my red flags, not yours. I think it will be OK if we're both working for them. They just seem to have had some bad experiences with other builders."

He reluctantly agreed to submit a proposal.

In the meantime, Fiona and I had come up with a timeline. "I've already missed out on a year of using my kitchen," she said. "I'm OK with missing Thanksgiving, but I don't want to miss *two* holidays. Just make sure it's done by Christmas." By now it was early fall. I would need a good six weeks to build and install the cabinetry, then the stone fabricator could come and make templates for counters. If we had our ducks in a row and there were no major changes to the plans, we had a reasonable chance of finishing by Christmas.

A few days later Rick sent his contract in duplicate. A week went by with no response. I was starting to worry about meeting the deadline, because my installation was dependent on preliminary work that would have to be done by a contractor. Rick called Bradley to ask whether they were planning to hire him.

"You sent me an eight-page contract," Bradley told him, as though this were unusually onerous for a lawyer. "I'm going to need a few days to read through it. I'll get it back to you as soon as I can."

The following week, Rick and his crew threw themselves into the job. They furred out the exterior wall and added insulation. They ran wiring and plumbing, roughed in the vent over the stove, finished drywall, and pulled up the 1970s floor tile.

Meanwhile, I was building the cabinets in my shop. The doors and drawers were going to be inset and hung on traditional, non-adjustable butt hinges, following the precedent of the original cabinets. In such cases I like to install the casework before I do the final trimming of doors and drawer faces, to ensure the best possible fit.

By mid-October I was ready for installation. Rick sent over one of his employees to help; we got the casework in on the first day. The next morning I arrived by myself with the doors and drawer faces in the back of my truck.

Oddly, Fiona was not alone this time. Bradley was with her.

"Hello," I said cheerily as I walked in with the first few doors. It felt good to be moving forward with the next phase of the job.

Fiona had an angry look in her eyes.

"Our friend Leo was over last night," Brad began. "He checked the cabinets and pointed out some problems." My stomach knotted. Problems?

"For one thing, the finish feels grainy. Also, he put a framing square on this corner and showed us that these faces are out of square. And he pointed out that there's a difference in shade between the left and right sides of the sink cabinet."

At this, Fiona shouted, "This is the first thing you see when you walk into the kitchen! How could you put two different colors of wood next to each other? I can't believe you would do this to us!"

What did she mean, "do this *to* us?" I forced myself to stay calm and began responding respectfully to their concerns one at a time. This was my standard finish, applied by hand – granted, not as satin-smooth as a sprayed conversion varnish, but I hadn't had a customer complain about it before. In kitchens, people are usually just handling their cabinets' hardware. Bradley stood by, listening. His expression suggested that he found my perspective reasonable.

Unfortunately his acquiescence was intolerable to Fiona. "Bradley!" she said. "What are you going to have Nancy do to correct this problem? I can't live with this finish." Suddenly she turned to me. "*These are custom cabinets!*" she shrieked.

Was I missing something? Was there some basic fact about my profession that I had failed to glean in 20 years of work at a variety of shops on two continents?

"The fact that these are custom cabinets means nothing other than that they're not from stock," I offered gently, by way of clarification, aware that any hint of defensiveness would likely inflame the situation. "There is no uniform standard among custom cabinetmakers. In fact, these cabinets are significantly more customized and of higher quality than what you would get from most makers of 'custom' cabinets, who would give you several choices to choose from but would not be matching the details of your kitchen's original cabinetry in anything like the detail I have."

She turned to her husband and snapped, "I knew I should have bought the upper-end cabinets from Lowe's." Turning to me, she said, "I forbid you to proceed with the kitchen until you have resolved this to our satisfaction. And from now on, please limit your comings and goings to the tradesman's door." With that she flew out of the room.

Could she be serious? Did she actually know anything about cabinetmaking? I sensed that the unfavorable comparison between my work and what she could have bought from a home improvement store was intended to hurt my feelings, but it was such a ridiculous comparison that I felt embarrassed for her, not myself. Brad and I looked at each other awkwardly. We needed Fiona to be part of the conversation.

He went looking for her, calling her name faintly. "Fiona? Honey? We need you to come back to the kitchen." He checked the butler's pantry. Then their bedroom. Finally, the basement. She was nowhere to be found. He dialed her cell phone. No answer. "Does she subject him to such treatment on a regular basis?" I wondered, summoning my inner interlocutor to keep me company, as I was suddenly feeling alone and vulnerable.

Since Fiona had disappeared, Brad and I discussed the outstanding issues together. The site conditions had resulted in our fitting the cabinets in such a way that the adjoining faces did not lie in exactly the same plane, I explained. I would scrape the joint and refinish it. Problem solved. The slight difference in shade between the left and right vertical frame members of the sink cabinet was due to the natural variation in the cherry. The face frames of cabinets are like frames of a picture, I said; while the shade difference might be noticeable now, it would disappear once the doors and drawers were in place.

But what were we to do without Fiona's blessing? She had been adamant that no further work was to be done, yet I had a truck loaded with doors and drawer faces ready to be fitted. The Billingsworths were due to leave for a week in Arizona; perhaps Fiona had been under a lot of stress at work. Some time away would give her a chance to cool down. Brad apologized for the inconvenience and agreed that perhaps the best thing would be for me to take the doors and drawer faces back to the shop and wait for their return. Of course, the deadline to complete the job would remain unchanged.

I was halfway back to my shop when my phone rang. "Nancy?" I recognized her tone. "What's going on? Brad said he asked you to leave. Why did he ask you to leave? We've got to get this kitchen done."

Indeed we did. I was beginning to appreciate that my sanity depended on wrapping up the job as expeditiously as possible.

My hand trembling, I steeled myself and responded calmly. "Fiona, Brad didn't 'ask' me to leave. That's a misrepresentation of what went on between us. We had a reasonable, businesslike discussion and agreed that we could not go further without your input. Brad looked all over the house for you and called your cell phone, but you were nowhere to be found. So we agreed that I would leave and wait to hear from you when you returned from Arizona. If you'd like me to come back this morning, I will, but that was not my understanding."

She seemed to relax now, realizing that I was not going to play the role she had assigned me. I turned around and drove the 30 miles back to their house. We met in the kitchen, where I repeated the explanation I had previously gone through with Brad.

"I guess I overreacted," she said. "My blood sugar was low."

I made a point of engaging her in friendly conversation while I set to fitting the doors. I genuinely wanted to get along with her, as I do with all my clients. We talked about the upcoming trip, her family in Sedona, the sequence of flights and car rides they would take on their whirlwind journey.

By late November the cabinets were finished, the counters installed. I'd kept two cabinets stored at my shop, away from any possible damage they might suffer at the construction site. One was a spice cabinet, a unique piece designed to resemble an antique; I was waiting for Fiona to make a decision about the type of glass she wanted for the doors. The other cabinet could not be installed until after the wall tile was in place.

Rick and his crew had just completed their part of the kitchen work and were cleaning up the jobsite to prep it for the tile installer, who was scheduled to start the next day. As Rick and his employee Melvin were heading out the door, Fiona called them back and asked if they would move the fridge into the dining room.

"I'm sorry, but my contract states that we don't move appliances," Rick told her. He and his employees had enough wear and tear on their backs and other joints without moving appliances. Besides, there was no telling when an old stove would belch out a trail of mouse droppings or a dilapidated fridge leak a stream of rusty water across an Oriental rug. Appliance and moving companies have the personnel and insurance coverage for that kind of work. Rick knew better than to get involved.

"It would really help me out if you would do this," she continued. "It's too heavy for me to move alone, and James will be here in the morning to start the tile. I don't want to ask him to do it. The fridge is on wheels. It's easy to move."

"Alright then," said Rick. "It's not that we don't want to be helpful. We're just wary of the kind of damage appliances can do."

She clapped her hands in grateful delight. "Thanks so much, guys."

Rick pulled the fridge toward him to gauge its weight. It was still full of food. "Melvin, grab that sheet of cardboard from the back of my truck. Let's put it down to protect the dining room floor, just in case." They moved the fridge, gave the floor a quick glance to make sure it was unscathed, and left. Relieved to be done, Rick wrote out his final bill that evening and emailed it to Brad.

The next morning when Rick checked his email, there was a message from Brad.

> Ric:
>
> The dining room floor is scratched. We are very unhappy and expect you to repair it before we pay your final balance.
>
> Brad

Rick called me with the news. "They say we scratched the floor. I'll go over today to take a look." James, the tile installer, let him in. There was a scratch; it followed the path of the fridge, apparently caused by a piece of grit trapped under the cardboard. But it was barely visible; you had to search to find it. Rick sent Brad a reply explaining that they had only moved the fridge as a favor to Fiona. He added that the scratch was minor; Fiona had told him that they planned to have the floor hand-scraped and refinished after the kitchen construction, which would take care of the damage.

The next morning he received a reply.

> Ric:
>
> I am an attorney! I familiarized myself thoroughly with your contract before signing it and assure you that I will not be making any further payments until you have repaired the floor to our satisfaction.
>
> Bradley Billingsworth

Swamped by the demands of several concurrent jobs, Rick decided to let the matter go for a few days.

Once the floor and wall tile had been grouted I returned to hang the last large cabinet. By then, Rick and his crew were working on a job in another town, so no one was available to give me a hand. Installing the cabinet by myself would be a challenge, but I'd dealt with worse. It was just something to get through.

I started with the pair of tall doors, which I had removed from the cabinet to reduce the bulk and weight. It was an icy morning; I nearly fell while making my way across Riverside Avenue, which was busy with morning traffic. I stashed the doors in the butler's pantry, leaning them carefully against the paneled wainscot and tucking a mover's blanket around them to protect their faces. Returning to the truck, I took a deep breath and braced myself. Even without doors, the cabinet was heavy for one person. I hefted it up. With the cabinet balanced against my right shoulder I negotiated my way across the street, then climbed cautiously up the front yard steps.

Avoiding the pile of steaming dog shit that had suddenly appeared in the middle of the path to the tradesman's entrance, I shuffled carefully along the slick ground. Thank God there were just four stairs up to the landing. I took them one at a time, working to stabilize myself on my leading foot as I lifted the rest of my body up, along with my precariously balanced load.

"Finally," I said to myself. "You're on the landing. Now just steady the carcase on the edge while you open the storm door."

Why did people need such heavy storm doors?

"That's it. Good. Pretend this is a Pilates exercise."

Despite being an exterior doorway, the opening was narrower than standard; apparently the tradesmen of yore hadn't needed much space to drop off their wares. Compounding the challenge of delivering anything larger than a sack of potatoes, the vestibule inside was scarcely large enough to turn around in. And once you did manage to turn around, you had to squeeze through another doorway to reach the kitchen proper.

"Prop the door open. Steady…steady. That's it. Now, carefully, protecting the cabinet's face with your body, ease slowly around the corner." Breathing a sigh of relief, I let the glass door off its stop and carried the cabinet into the pantry, where I placed it against the blanketed doors.

My shoulder ached from being poked for so long by the cabinet's sharp corner, and my right palm, now bright red, was temporarily paralyzed in a freakish contortion. But I'd been dreading this delivery for days, and I was relieved to have pulled it off without mishap.

As I walked back out to get my tools, I noticed a Post-it with a scribbled message that had been stuck to the door while I was inside: "FIONA IS SICK. FLU?" "Please, no," I thought, wondering whether I would be permitted to work that day while silently scolding myself for being so selfish as to think about my schedule when my client was under the weather. To finish the work I would need to make noise, running my compressor and using the chop saw to miter the crown. Oh well; I would get through as much as I could.

And then she appeared, a vision in white velour. "I'm sorry to hear you're not feeling well," I told her, sincerely. "I recently had the same thing – sore throat, muscle aches, exhaustion. I'll keep my use of the compressor to a minimum so you can rest."

Her face assumed that familiar tightness.

We exchanged a few words about hardware for the potato bin: Where would she like me to position the pulls? I pointed out the cabinet and doors in the butler's pantry, awaiting installation. She nodded in acknowledgement.

"Y'know, I gotta tell ya, I'm not sure these pulls are going to work." At that she stopped herself. Things were obviously headed in a bad direction. My stomach knotted. But then, reprieve – at least, temporarily. "I feel like hell. I'm afraid I'm not going to be much use to you today." I told her that was fine; I could postpone installing the hardware on the potato bin. "Brad'll be by at 10:30 to bring me some soup."

After she went upstairs I tiptoed into the dining room to examine the floor. As Rick had said, it took some effort to locate the scratch. But the scratch was there, and unfortunately it went across the grain of the floorboards for part of its length; a scratch that shallow running parallel with the grain would have been invisible. I pulled a touch-up stick from my toolbox and rubbed some into the scratch, inching along on my hands and knees. Instantly the area around it darkened, indicating that the finish had worn off long ago. I looked across the floor. From my low vantage point I could see that its surface was a maze of scratches from the dogs' claws.

I was taping a sheet of protective material onto the stone counter when the dogs began howling. Brad must have arrived. Moments later he appeared, said hello, and sprinted upstairs to check on his wife. Dimly, I made out the occasional weakly uttered word. "Nancy...cabinet...ask...damaged."

When Brad returned there was something frenetic about his demeanor. He glanced surreptitiously into the pantry, then the kitchen, spun around, and retreated to the stairway. "I can't see it," I heard him whisper up the stairs, as though trying to keep a secret. "IT'S IN THE PANTRY," she barked from the bedroom. Brad returned, focused his gaze on the cabinet, then on me, and with palpable distress informed me that Fiona would like me to remove the cabinet and doors from the premises, as she was sure they would get damaged.

Damaged? What possible harm could befall the cabinet in their house, now that the rest of the kitchen work had been done?

"I think she wants to make sure the cabinets are protected from me!" he chuckled in a feeble attempt to ease our mutual awkwardness in the face of his wife's absurd demand. "She isn't up to the noise and disturbance of having you install the cabinet today. She feels too sick." Feeling sorry for him, now, I said that of course I would remove the cabinet; it would be no problem at all.

"Is there anything else we have to discuss?" he asked.

"Only the elephant in the room," I replied in a lowered voice. "I heard about the messages between you and Rick, and I would rather talk about the floor than try to avoid the issue." I showed him the spots I had touched up, explaining that the oil was only visible because the floor had been effectively stripped of finish by years of canine wear. As I spoke, I imagined her upstairs, ear against a glass pressed to the floor, despite her weakened condition. In voices just loud enough to be audible between us, Brad and I discussed a couple of possible fixes before he had to get ready to return to the office. "You're right," he said. "The scratch is minor and will be removed when we get the floor refinished."

"Just one thing," he added, turning back toward me and pointing at the floor. "Do *not* – I repeat, DO NOT – talk about the elephant in the room with Fiona. She gets very emotional about these things."

By the time I was ready to leave, the temperature had risen and it was raining. I repeated my delivery in reverse, studiously dabbing the beads of water off the cabinet and each of the doors as I delivered them to the safety of my truck.

Rick called that evening. "I can't believe you talked me into working for those people," he said. "Thank goodness they only owe me six hundred dollars. It's obvious they're never going to pay me. If I never go back there, it will be the best six hundred dollars I ever spent."

A week later, Fiona was feeling well enough to endure my presence. Christmas break had begun. We were down to the wire. By this time I was deeply traumatized by my interactions with the Billingsworths and reluctant to enter their home by myself without a third-party witness. What crime might they accuse me of? My friend Lulu, a professor at a university in Chicago, was in town to spend the break with her partner. I begged her to accompany me as my helper.

Bradley drove home from his office to let us in. Although someone had clearly just been chopping vegetables – a neat pile of minced onions and peppers glistened on the counter in a still-life worthy of a Dutch master – there was no sign of Fiona. Together, Lulu and I hung the cabinet. While I screwed the hinges into place she told me about the picnic her department had held to welcome new faculty members at the start of the semester. The lone native Midwesterner, she'd shown up with 5 gallons of mayonnaise-laden potato salad, only to discover that her colleagues, all of them credit-card thin, "don't actually eat; they just nibble."

I knew the Billingsworths would be leaving at the start of January for a semester in Scotland, where Brad would be guest-lecturer at a law school. I hoped that Fiona would make a decision about the glass for her spice cabinet doors so that I could hang the thing and be done before their departure. Although they only owed me a balance of $500 on their contract, I needed the money. Besides, I try hard to stay on good terms with all my clients, no matter how challenging a job may occasionally become. It was a gorgeous kitchen and I was proud of my part in creating it. I wanted to get photos for my portfolio.

My emails and phone calls about the glass for the spice cabinet went unanswered. On January 7th they flew away for the semester.

In June I received an email message from Fiona: "I've found some glass I love and had it cut to the dimensions you provided. It's ready for you to pick up at the Martin County Glass Center."

I drove to Martin County, wondering why she had chosen such a faraway source for glass she could have purchased closer to home. It was a beautiful day, and I tried to focus on the verdant landscape instead of suspecting that my time was being wasted intentionally. Soon, surely, this job would be over.

That evening, glass in hand, I called Fiona about installing it in the doors and hanging the cabinet. "Sure!" she replied, apparently refreshed by her Scottish sojourn. "I'm so ready to have this kitchen finished. It has taken far too long."

"May I bring my photographer with me to shoot the kitchen?" I asked, hoping to kill two birds with one stone.

"Um…no," she replied. "I don't think we want to have the kitchen photographed. Bradley and I are very private people." Well, that was disappointing, though I had to admit I was not completely surprised, based on her behavior to date. I should never have let her know how eager I was to get photos.

I arrived to find her holding the side door open for me before I even had a chance to knock. "Gotta run. Emergency trip to the lingerie store! I've left your check on the sideboard in the entryway."

"Well," I thought with a sense of relief. "That's decent of her." Maybe I'd been misreading her.

I brought in my tools and got started. I draped a thick blanket over the counter where I would be working, set a toolbox on top of it and stacked several books I had brought to support the spice cabinet at the necessary height. I marked the position of the studs on the hanging rail and drilled through the cabinet back, then used a diamond bit to drill through the porcelain wall tile. Once the cabinet was hung I installed the glass in the doors and screwed the hinges in place. At last my work was done.

I carried the tools and blanket out to my truck and swept up the dust I'd made. Once everything was cleared away, I stepped into the entryway to get the check. Apart from a vase of flowers and a couple of envelopes sitting on a mail order catalog, the sideboard was bare. I looked under the stack of mail, then between the pieces, in case someone had inadvertently placed one or more of them on top of the check. Nothing.

I went back to my truck and got my point-and-shoot camera. If she was going to persist in her game of cat and mouse, this mouse was going to get some cheese. It would be a poorly lit snapshot of an unstaged scene, but at least I'd have a record of my work.

"Fiona," I wrote by email that evening, "I hung the spice cabinet but couldn't find the check. May I stop by tomorrow to pick it up?"

"Oops!" she wrote back. "I must have forgotten. Yes, come by at 10."

To my relief, she was there and handed me a check.

Don't Call Me Boss

FOR A short time in the late 1990s I tried to grow my business, as small business owners are typically expected to do. I had as much work as I could handle and was turning away potential jobs from people unwilling to wait for an opening in my schedule. "Time to hire an employee," advised a couple of friends.

I took on the role of employer with some hesitation. I had always identified with my own bosses and tried to see things from their perspective. After all, I was working in their business and only had a job because they needed someone to do it. Which is to say that I was never the kind of employee who tried to subvert the system. If things seemed like they could be done better, I might bring this up with my boss. But in the end, as an employee, I had the luxury of leaving. On the other hand, by the time I was poised to hire someone, I'd spent a few years in academe. I'd dipped my toes in John Stuart Mill and Adam Smith. The authors I found most impressive were Marx, Ruskin, and a few contemporary critics of capitalism. I graduated convinced that most business people were out to exploit their workers, and I was determined not to be that kind of boss.

Richard was an excellent woodworker in his 40s. We'd known each other as fellow members of the local woodworking scene. He had worked for one of my competitors but quit after not receiving a raise in a decade. Later he took a job at a factory in a nearby city, but he hated the commute. He called in response to my "Help Wanted" ad.

Richard did not have a good word to say about any of his former employers. When I asked him for references he gave me the name of a personal friend. No doubt you're thinking this was a bad sign. Yeah, I had that same thought. So just to be on the safe side, I called my friendly competitor and asked his opinion on Richard as an employee. "He's a great craftsman, though not the fastest worker," he told me. I knew Richard's work. The man was good. And I was a decent, kind person. I felt cautiously optimistic that we would get along just fine.

I hired him at $15 an hour, which was more than I was paying myself and more than the going rate at most comparable shops. He was certainly worth more considering his skills, but $15 was already a stretch for my business. At the factory job he'd be leaving if he came to work with me, he was making just under $20, so I wanted to do what I could. Every dollar I paid him would cost my business about $1.50 after liability insurance and worker's compensation premiums, unemployment dues, and similar legally mandated expenses. (Forget about paid vacations and public holidays, health insurance, and other so-called "benefits," none of which my microenterprise could afford. I had only ever had such luxuries from a woodworking employer once; most small custom furniture and cabinetmaking shops just can't provide them.) As long as we were productive and I had enough orders to keep us in billable hours, paying Richard at this rate should not pose a problem. I needed help; he wanted to work with me. And I was confident that I could find no one in town who was more qualified, let alone available.

His first project in my shop was to build and help install a set of kitchen cabinets. He took almost twice as long as I had allowed in my estimate, but he was new to my shop, so it was only fair to allow for a learning curve. No matter how experienced you are, every new shop has its quirks: different machinery, idiosyncratic methods preferred by your employer. I just needed to be patient and show some faith.

"Richard, this is beautiful work," I told him. "But I need you to up the pace a bit." He said he would.

When I added up his hours at the end of his third project I saw that he was still taking too much time. I felt a genuine obligation to try to work things out, because he'd left a job that was more secure and far better paid, albeit one he'd said "killed another piece of my soul with each passing day."

Unfortunately for us both, Richard did not seem to know any other pace. If things didn't change, I was going to be in serious trouble.

"Richard," I said to him. "You're consistently taking on average twice as much time as I've allowed for."

"You don't know how to estimate," he replied. "Remember: I was the manager at a furniture factory. I know how to estimate."

"OK, then," I answered hopefully, wondering whether my experiences at a couple of tightly run shops in England had left me with unrealistic expectations when it came to productivity. "Let's do this: From now on,

I will show you the drawings and specs before I write a proposal, and you can tell me how much time you think I should allow."

Unfortunately he routinely exceeded even his own labor estimates.

Just after Thanksgiving I had to face the brutal truth that in four months of employing Richard I had gone almost $6,000 into debt. We were digging a hole that would only get deeper. I saw no way to keep it up without ending in bankruptcy.

"I'm sick to death of your whining," my adviser at the small business resource center said at our next meeting. "You're not running a social service organization. Richard has skills. He's eminently employable. You have to let him go."

It was a wrenching decision that left me sleepless for nights. The man prided himself on his work. He lived alone, as did I at the time, so there was no partner's income to help out. And obviously my name was going to be dragged through the mud along with those of all his previous employers. On top of this, Christmas was just around the corner. Only a heartless bastard would lay someone off at that time of year, and I was not a heartless bastard. I could already hear Richard talking to his friends. Option A: "Can you believe she let me go right before Christmas? What kind of person does that?" Option B: "She kept me in the dark and let me enjoy the holidays as if everything was fine, then kicked me to the curb on January second. Hey, thanks for the 'Happy New Year,' Nancy Hiller." But unlike Option A, Option B would put me around $1,000 deeper in debt.

My business adviser was right. At least Richard, as an employee, would be able to get some government assistance. If I lost my business, I would not have access to such aid. A week before Christmas I sat down with Richard and delivered the news. It was one of the hardest conversations I have ever had – well, less a conversation than the dropping of a bomb (though the bomb was surely not completely unexpected). He faced me in stony silence before thanking me for the talk, which was gracious of him.

I did not want to have another employee ever again.

A Case of Mistaken Identity

ACROSS THE alley from a house where I once worked was a yard where an elderly woman with dementia spent her days. The privacy fence around the yard was 8' high, so I couldn't see inside. But based on the rest of the house, an imposing limestone foursquare with a carved entryway and elegant landscaping, I knew that the backyard must be charming. I pictured French doors leading out to a patio of bluestone pavers beneath a wisteria-draped arbor. Glazed clay pots held crotons and bougainvillea that the owners of this fine home kept alive under grow lights each winter. A pebbled path extended from the patio to the back fence, dividing the perfectly manicured lawn into symmetrical rectangles edged with neatly mulched flower beds.

My customer knew the homeowners, Penelope and Derick Brace, who shared the house with their two sons and Derick's mother, Mrs. Bracegirdle, the woman in the backyard. They had moved to Bloomington from New Orleans. I occasionally saw the boys leaving for school; they were always neatly dressed and well behaved. The Braces – my customer had told me that Penelope made Derick legally change his surname before she would marry him because she did not want any child of hers to be teased for the name "Bracegirdle" – were obviously a lovely family.

Old Mrs. Bracegirdle was wheeled out to this haven every morning, weather permitting. Penelope parked her in the shade of a dogwood tree whose limbs reached over the top of the fence, sharing their lush white blooms with all passersby. The alley offered a pleasant route through our town's most prestigious historic neighborhood, so it saw a lot of pedestrian traffic. Graduate students and professors took the alley to and from campus; it was also a favorite place for young mothers pushing strollers.

After a couple of days across from Mrs. Bracegirdle I realized why her daughter-in-law wanted to get her as far away as possible. Ol' Bracie was a talker. She chattered nonstop. How could you focus on anything with all that jabbering in the background? Fortunately, most of my work was inside my customer's house, so I was spared. But every time I came outside to trim a door on my portable workbench I was privy to the banter. Far more troubling than her excessive volubility was that dementia had robbed her of any social filters. She unwittingly shared everything with the neighborhood.

She spent a lot of time on the phone – or maybe she just thought she was on the phone and was reciting conversations from years before; it was hard to say. "Oh my God," she'd say in a tone of deep concern, followed by some response that was too muffled by the fence to make out. She often conversed with an old friend in another state; they complained a lot about their husbands. "I don't know why he took a job in this godforsaken town," I once heard her say. "Put the kibosh on my career, that's for damn sure." After a pause while she listened to her friend's response I'd hear a drawn-out "Ohhh" of sympathy. There'd be another pause, followed by a thoughtful "OK." Her tone was so expressive that I found myself wondering what terrible thing her friend's husband had done. Had he gone to prison? Had an affair? Of course, all of this referred to events in the distant past. By the time I encountered Mrs. Bracegirdle she'd been a widow for at least two decades.

Every so often I'd hear her sobbing like a baby and my heart would go out to her. She'd lost her husband to cancer. It was a slow death, and painful, but he'd been a trouper. She had cared for him 'round the clock, lying beside him every night in the bed they'd shared since they were newly married. "Don't leave me," she'd begged. "I am nothing without you." But of course he died anyway. The memorial was a grand affair, held in one of New Orleans' great cathedrals. Everyone who was anyone attended, wishing to pay their respects to one of the city's most beloved public servants. I couldn't fathom why she referred to New Orleans as a godforsaken town, but we all have our idiosyncrasies. Perhaps she'd grown up in New York or Boston, so any place in the South was bound to be a letdown.

Fortunately, not all of what I overheard was so grim. Sometimes she laughed – and hers was no shy titter. She'd cackle with such hearty delight that the sound never failed to make me smile. The old woman must have some stories, I thought, feeling a growing fondness for her even though we'd never so much as said hello. I calculated that she must have been born in the 1920s, lived through the Depression, and served as a WAC in WWII. She was a member of the greatest generation.

A CASE OF MISTAKEN IDENTITY 117

One day the sky turned suddenly dark and a heavy rain blew over. Apparently Mrs. Bracegirdle's daughter-in-law was running on the treadmill, music blasting through her headphones; she was oblivious to her charge outside. The dogwood tree offered no real cover. I dashed out to throw a tarp over my miter saw and heard Mrs. Bracegirdle prattling away as usual. Far from being upset by the downpour, she seemed to be having the time of her life. "Yeeeeeeeeeeee!" she shrieked joyously. "Ha ha ha ha ha!" She whistled the tune from the Andy Griffiths Show, sang "do re me fa so la ti do," then broke into a heartbreaking rendition of *Un Bel Di* from Madame Butterfly. Obviously the poor girl thought she was in the shower. I marveled at the diversity of her bath-time repertoire. Andy Griffiths and Madame Butterfly? The more I heard, the more I wished I could meet her.

A few days later, my work was finished. I stayed late to pack up my truck. Dusk had fallen, and Mrs. Bracegirdle was making sweet cooing sounds, as though she were putting a baby to bed. I heard Penelope come out to fetch her. No sooner had Penelope taken hold of the wheelchair's handles than Mrs. Bracegirdle responded with an inarticulate exclamation – a sound so violent and unfeminine that I can only call it a cross between a retch and a growl. She then began to scream bloody murder, as though she was being attacked. "Wow," I thought. "Penelope must have the patience of a saint to put up with such behavior from her mother-in-law."

When I returned a few days later to pick up a check from my customer, Penelope was putting out her trash. "Hi!" I called, running over to shake her hand. "I've been working in your neighbor's kitchen for a couple of weeks and I must say I've enjoyed hearing your mother-in-law through the fence. She's quite a talker."

Penelope rolled her eyes. "That's not my mother-in-law," she said. "It's my husband's stupid parrot, a yellow-naped Amazon named Pedro."

In a flash I saw it all. The wheelchair was a birdcage, the cooing at dusk a bird's instinctive self-readying for sleep. As for singing in the warm downpour, what more natural response could there be from a bird born for life in a tropical rainforest?

"I detest that bird," Penelope continued as I was recalibrating my view of their charming household, the likely truth behind the phone conversations beginning to sink in, "but Derick dotes on the thing. He's had that bird since it hatched from an egg, years before we met. You can be certain that if I'd been around, I would never have let him buy it. I went to graduate school in New Orleans to become an opera singer and I can't even practice in my own house because that goddamn bird mimics me relentlessly. He parrots every melody, knows every line. As for having a conversation on the phone with a girlfriend, forget it. Everything I say is recorded in the pea-sized brain of that flying rat, and I have no control over what he might repeat."

She glanced angrily at the house. "That bird hates me. Derick expects me to take care of it when he goes away on business, but it bit my hand when I tried to feed it on the last trip, so I told him 'no more.' For years I've been begging him to sell it or give it away. You wouldn't have any interest in taking it, would you? We're moving in a few weeks. This could be a good time to make a break."

I thought about it for a few days and told her that I'd love to adopt Pedro, provided that Derick agreed to it. The bird was such a character. She assured me that they'd discussed it and he was finally ready to let his pet go to another home. "Be here at 4 next Thursday to take him."

Derick was helping the movers load a truck when I arrived. "I'm here to pick up Pedro," I said. "What?" he asked, completely unaware of Penelope's arrangement. His face fell as he turned and rushed back inside the house. "I can't believe you did this, Penelope!" I heard him shout in the kitchen. "I know how you operate, but I would never have expected *this*: the *day* we're moving, with the truck almost loaded and no time left for discussion."

"Oh my God," I said when he returned. "I don't need to take your bird! Penelope told me you'd agreed to this. But the last thing I want to do is separate the two of you if you're not OK with that."

"This is how my wife does things," he said, tears running down his face. "It's for the best. I'll never hear the end of it if I keep him. Just take him. And please give him a good life."

My heart ached for the man. He helped me put Pedro's cage on the front seat of my truck. Leaning through the passenger's-side window, he looked at Pedro and whispered, "take care of yourself, old friend."

On the drive home Pedro whistled the tune from the Andy Griffiths Show over and over again. When I parked the truck in the driveway and opened the door, he looked at me and said, "Derick! What're you gonna do about the goddamn bird?"

A CASE OF MISTAKEN IDENTITY

Ten years later, Pedro laid an egg.[1]

---

[1] "Cute story," you're probably thinking. "But what's it doing in this book?" I thought about adding the subtitle: "A Fable Regarding the Perils of Inference and Assumption," but that would have given too much away.

The Value of Nothing: A Play in Four Acts

1. On the Importance of Conjunctions

A few years ago I met one of our town's most respected figures: a husband and father who has held several elected public offices and devoted his career to the cause of social justice. As we shook hands he said, "I understand that your work is very good, but not very cheap."
"But?" I wondered, biting my tongue.

2. The Value of Nothing, Part One: The Magician's Act

Guy and Poppy were retired business professors who had traveled the world. And judging by what I saw as they showed me around their home during my first visit, they'd brought a good bit of it back home with them.
They had been referred to me by a contractor who assured them I'd be ideal for their project. "We just bought a reproduction of a piece of sculpture," Poppy wrote in her introductory email.

> The first photo shows the original swan at the S. Museum, and the second is the reproduction in the museum shop, just like the one we have. We need a stand to display the statue. Please give us a call if you're interested in helping us with this.

It wasn't the type of job I ordinarily do, but because they'd been referred to me by a contractor I like and respect, I called Poppy and arranged a meeting.
Their house was stunning: a classic of modernist style, inside and out – not that I would have guessed as I pulled up to the windowless façade,

a gray stone rectangle apparently modeled on a freight container. But no sooner had I set foot inside than the scales dropped from my eyes. The other exterior walls were glass, spectacular in the house's wooded setting.

Works of art filled the interior. Here a Coptic embroidery flanked by a pair of Yoruba masks, there a threesome of Warhol prints. A 16th-century Japanese screen formed a movable divider between the living room and the kitchen, itself a perfectly preserved marvel of original 1960s design. Clearly these people had excellent taste and understood the value of art and craft. I made myself a mental note to send the contractor a letter of thanks for the referral.

They showed me the swan, a plaster cast of the original statue carved in marble, and explained their ideas for how to display it.

"See how the neck has been extended in the reproduction so it sits square," Guy pointed out. "The swan's tail is on the same level as the neck. We'd like to have a base in which the swan's chest sits down inside, with the neck and head hanging over the edge, as in the original sculpture. Also, we don't just want an empty box for a base. That would be a waste of space. We could really do with some additional storage. I was thinking perhaps a couple of compartments with doors. No visible hinges or pulls, though; we do want it to look like a base for a sculpture, not a cabinet. Maybe zebrawood? Oh, and if you could put it on hidden wheels, that would be wonderful; that way we can move it around on the carpet whenever we feel the need for a change of scenery. We're getting a bit long in the tooth to be lifting heavy objects." He glanced affectionately at his wife. "Aren't we, Poppet?"

Poppy took me into the study and fired up her computer to show me photos of the original frieze of which the swan was a fragment. She found the folder of pictures from the trip and furrowed her brow in concentration as she scrolled through thumbnail images.

"We're getting close now," she assured me after what seemed an eternity. She clicked on an image to open it at full size. Suddenly the screen filled with a picture of a misshapen purple posterior that put me in mind of Barney, the PBS dinosaur. "Oh dear!" said Poppy, "Wrong picture. Hang on." She clicked forward to another, this one leaving no doubt that the posterior in question was Guy's. "Guy had a very unfortunate fall on the steps of our hotel," she said matter of factly. I blushed. "I had to get photos for the insurance claim." She clicked on. "Ah! Here we are."

"We had a fellow at the university do some work for us last year," she told me after closing the folder. "He had every problem in the book:

financial troubles, health troubles…. I think his great-uncle also died during our project. In any case, the small job he did for us took two full years. So you can understand we're not too keen on asking him about this one."

I took some measurements, made a few notes, and said goodbye. While driving back to the shop, I thought about the project. These people obviously had strong ideas about how the base for the sculpture should look and function, yet they knew my specialty was period-style furniture, not museum-worthy display cases. There would definitely need to be some back-and-forth discussion, which probably meant a couple more visits to their home, half an hour's drive away from my office, in addition to the time I'd spend on research and drawing. And all for a very small job. Poppy's mention of the fellow from the university was a little concerning. I'm familiar with the phenomenon of the full-time, full-benefits employee who avails him- or herself of institutional facilities after hours. Unburdened by trifles such as shop rent, insurance, and similar expenses that full-time business people have to cover, such moonlighters can do some serious undercutting when it comes to price. In doing so they perpetuate unrealistic notions of what it costs to make things, which often leads their customers to see us professionals as engaging in daylight robbery.

For a moment I felt myself falling into a familiar doom-portending spiral. Why must people ask me to pull a rabbit out of a hat? "Give us an estimate to design and build this thing. Sure, you have precious little to go on, we have no idea what such a thing should cost, and you understand that we want something that will knock our socks off, though of course, as retirees, we have to watch every penny. But you come highly recommended. We're confident you can do it."

I stopped myself. These were sophisticated people. "Just be straight with them," I told myself. "Trust the process."

Still, to hedge my bets, I thought it prudent to ask whether they had even the vaguest budget in mind.

"Dear Guy and Poppy," I wrote the night following our initial meeting.

> "I thoroughly enjoyed meeting you and seeing your fabulous home. I was writing a formal proposal for your job when it occurred to me that I should ask whether you have a budget in mind. In cases where designing a custom piece is such an integral part of the work I am proposing, I cannot give a fixed price; there is too little information available at this stage. So I usually submit

a design proposal based on my design rate of $75 per hour.

However, if you have a budget in mind, please let me know, and I will take that into consideration as we go through the design process."

Poppy replied 10 minutes later. "We really don't have a budget in mind, Nancy. Can you give us some options?"

I spent an hour methodically jotting down all the steps that would likely be required to design, then build, two distinct variations on the theme. Then I estimated the cost of the labor and materials involved in each one. The next evening I wrote back, summarizing my results.

> Dear Poppy and Guy,
> In cases such as yours, where the overall scale of a job is relatively small but I have no real way of knowing how much time will be required to design the piece, I make an allowance for design time. 'Design time' includes time spent meeting, drawing, making mock-ups, finish samples, conducting any research into materials that may be necessary, and discussing the job with you. In this case I think three to six hours would be more than enough. This would translate to somewhere between $225 and $450.
>
> Once I have a simple drawing to indicate how the piece is to be constructed, of which materials, with which finish, etc., I will have a basis for estimating the cost to build it. Depending on variables, which are still considerable at this point, the construction could cost anywhere from $950 to $2750. I know, it's a huge range, but I can get much closer as the design work proceeds. On the other hand, if I have an idea of your preferred budget, I can simply tailor the design accordingly.

To cover myself, I threw in an extra paragraph.

> Because I operate a full-time business on which my livelihood depends, and because I am using equipment and a facility for which I am 100 percent responsible, my charges for such work are likely to be higher than those of a person working at the university who can do the work using university-owned

equipment, in his or her spare time. Apologies for this explanation. I hope it will be helpful.

I am certainly interested in doing this work for you. If you would like to proceed, please let me know where, along the budget spectrum, you would like your job to land, and I will gladly write up a formal proposal.

Two days later I received a reply. "Well, you have startled us a bit, Nancy," Poppy wrote. "The higher price you've proposed is twice the price we paid for the piece itself, including the shipping, and that seems awfully high."

I don't know who ended up building the base for the swan.

3. The Value of Nothing, Part Two: Artistic License

> 6/3/11 3:35 PM
> Inquiry
>
> Dear Ms. Hiller,
>
> I have admired your quartersawn oak desk with inlaid bumble bees and am interested in possibly commissioning one like it. Will you please tell me what it would cost for such a desk with a top measuring 36" by 60"?
>
> Dr. X
>
>
> 6/3/11 8:18 PM
> Re: Inquiry
>
> Dear Dr. X,
>
> Thank you for your inquiry. I designed and built the desk that you found on my website in 2004. The desk's construction is traditional, using mortise-and-tenon and dovetail joinery, and the inlay is all done by hand. I keep detailed records of the labor and materials that go into every piece. Based on today's material costs and my current shop rate, the desk would be $5,250 plus sales

tax. Of course the design could be modified to suit whatever budget you might have in mind.

I would be delighted to discuss this with you by phone or in person.

Sincerely,
Nancy Hiller

6/17/11 7:04 AM
Following up

Dear Dr. X,

I am writing to confirm that you received my reply to your inquiry on June 3. Every so often I learn that an email message I sent was not received. I would be mortified if you thought that I had not responded promptly. Please will you let me know whether you received my message?

Sincerely,
Nancy

6/24/11 10:09 AM
Re: Following up

I did receive your quote. It is considerably higher than the prices I got from H Furniture and F Cabinets to build the same desk. Both H and F use tenon joinery and dovetails so we have nothing further to talk about.

4. Looking Over the Edge

10/11/03 5:47 AM
Request for a meeting

Dear Ms. Hiller,

I admired your Edwardian hallstand in *Fine Woodworking* and was thrilled to see that you are located in Bloomington, which is less than two hours away from my home. I have taken a number of wood-working classes and am seriously considering leaving my corporate job to become a professional furniture maker. I would greatly appreciate an opportunity to meet you and tour your shop. Would this be possible?

Sincerely,
G.P.

10/11/03 6:46 PM
Re: Request for a meeting

Dear G,

I would be happy to meet you and discuss your plans, but first I'd like to set you straight regarding the nature of my shop. There is nothing to "tour." My current shop – the nicest one I've ever had – is in a utility building of about 1,000 square feet located on a cattle farm. It is a single space; you can see everything from the front door. I am there most days, so just let me know some days and times that would be good for you.

Nancy

    G arrived at the scheduled time and we had a nice conversation. He worked for an international company headquartered in Indianapolis. He was probably around 40, married, and told me that while he valued his job and did not take the pay, security, or benefits for granted, he was sorely tempted to try his hand at furniture making full-time. "I've taken a class in furniture making as a business," he told me, "so I would have no trouble telling a prospective client that I had to charge $1,500 for a coffee table."
    "The question is not so much whether you have the guts to charge what it costs to build a piece," I replied, "but whether the prospective client is able – and more important, willing – to pay it."
    I gave him what insights I could about the realities of professional furniture making based on my experience, and told him that in my opinion he was in an enviable situation: securely employed, with paid vacations and other benefits that afforded him the freedom to do work he wanted to do in his spare time. I told him to feel free to keep in touch about his plans, but he didn't, so I have no idea whether he ever took the plunge.

Daniel

SHORTLY AFTER I moved into my current shop in rural Monroe County I started sleeping there as well. It was late fall, 2004, and I needed to get out of a relationship that had become impossible.

I moved my bed, a poplar pencil-post made as a prototype years before, into what should have been the finishing room. Because the shop had no heating or plumbing at the time, I bought a portable electric radiator and carried a jug out to the standpipe by the road to get water. An empty drywall bucket made a handy toilet on nights when it was too cold to go outside. I concentrated on seeing my new arrangement as an adventure.

The rest of my plan for the acre I'd acquired with the proceeds from selling my home in town had been to build a small house to rent out. My boyfriend, a general contractor, had constructed the shell of the house by the time our relationship ended. I got a mortgage,[1] paid him for his work, and calculated the income I would need now that I was apparently going to be the house's occupant. I saw no way of making ends meet on the revenue I could generate through my labor alone. At 45, I was less than enthusiastic about having to share my space with a roommate, as I had off and on for years. But if I could keep enough orders coming in – a not-in-

---

[1] It is far more difficult to obtain a mortgage when you're a single person, especially a woman, and self-employed – even more so when your income is modest. I have had mortgage officers laugh at me (literally) when I applied for a loan. I could have gone to an independent broker and signed up for one of those great deals available before The Crash (you know, the "interest-only payment/no principal!" kind, or the kind that let you borrow 110 percent of your property's value), but I wanted to stick with a local bank. I got a mortgage thanks to my neighbor, Elizabeth Cox-Ash, a loan officer at a regional bank; because she knew me and understood that I would do anything to avoid jeopardizing my home, she took a chance on me with an in-house loan.

significant challenge in a locale where skilled woodworkers are a dime a dozen – I figured I'd be able to pay an employee, cover the business operating expenses, and make enough to live on. The added bonus was that if things worked out, I would be giving someone a job. I could beat myself up until the cows came home about my disastrous first experience as an employer, but at least I knew I'd done all I could to treat my first employee well.

I called a woodworking friend who always seemed to have a few people working in his shop and asked whether he could spare one, at least part-time.

"This is a happy coincidence," he answered. "I took Daniel on expecting to get a huge commission that would have kept him busy for a year, but the job fell through and he needs more hours than I can give him. It would be a dream come true if you just hired him full-time."

We quickly developed a decent working relationship. Daniel, who was in his mid-20s, had a good range of skills and picked up new ones in a flash. He was not only meticulous, but productive: a rare combination. Most of the shops I'd worked in had valued the latter over the former. They all produced work of quality, but in my professional experience up to that time, the pursuit of excellence for its own sake had been considered an unaffordable luxury.

One of the first jobs I gave him was a toy cabinet for a client's daughter, essentially an armoire: four doors, salvaged hardware, simple trim. He'd finished the piece, aside from the crown, which was long enough that it would take both of us to steady it while one of us nailed it in place.

"Hold it right there," I said from the third step of the ladder. I pressed the trigger on the brad gun, moved to the next spot, and pressed again, working my way along the moulding's length.

"Shit!" he yelled.

"Ha ha," I groaned, knowing better than to fall for this expression of pain. The guy was constantly provoking some reaction from me; whatever my response, it gave him a chance to impersonate me, an art he'd secretly mastered during his first week in my employ. His wicked studies left me guffawing until I cried. How had I lived so many years without realizing how much I resembled a chicken racing from a butcher's knife when I freaked out during a complex glue-up? Was my laugh really that much like a hyena's? By now I was on to his antics and wary of taking the bait. Still, just to make sure, I asked "You *are* kidding, right?"

"No," he moaned. His hand was stuck fast to the cabinet.

"Oh my God!" I shrieked. "What do we do? Hang on!"

As though he had any choice.

My mind raced. What if the brad had gone through his bone? This craftsman might lose the use of a hand due to my stupidity. Unthinkable. I had no idea what to do. Rush him to the hospital? But he was attached to the cabinet. Call an ambulance?

It was winter. The ground was covered in snow. I raced outside and grabbed a handful. At least the cold would help with the pain while I figured out what to do next.

I ran back in to find him liberated.

"How did you get your hand off?"

"I just pulled my finger out of the nail," he replied. "It was a weird sensation, but I didn't see any alternative."

"Go to the doctor right now. Then go home for the rest of the afternoon," I told him, concerned about the possibility of infection. "I'll cover the cost of the doctor's visit and pay you for the rest of the day."

"Nah," he said. "I'm fine. I'll keep working."

The high point of our time together was a trip to Washington, D.C., in the summer of 2006. It started with a call from a prospective client who'd found my website through a search for "1930 sink."

"How would you like to go on an all-expenses-paid working trip to our nation's capital?" I asked Daniel after that call. Of course at that point the job was just a fantasy. However, if it did come through, I would want to do the installation to ensure that all of the parts went together according to my design. He had never been to Washington and said he was game.

After a preliminary visit to meet the prospective customers, Amy and Martin, to discuss their kitchen, which had fallen victim to some DIY "improvements" in the 1990s, I sent a proposal and was excited to hear that they wanted to hire us. The cabinets would be made of hard maple with inset doors on traditional butt hinges. The drawer faces, too, would be inset. They wanted custom wooden shelf supports based on those they'd seen in an antique cupboard; that would be a fun detail to fabricate. One wall would have a 9' run of cabinets housing integrated refrigerator and freezer drawers beneath a solid cherry counter; above would be built-ins up to the ceiling. Of course the ceiling, floor, and adjacent wall were all seriously out of level; to compensate for this while keeping our trim to a minimum for the cleanest look, we would build the upper cabinets for this wall in parts, assembling them during the installation on site. Only after we'd finished installing the casework would we be able to fit the doors and drawer faces.

I scheduled the installation for the two last weeks in June. There would be no wiggle room on the far end because I had to drive to Kentucky on July 2 to teach a cabinetmaking class. Daniel built the cabinets and I built the counter, fitting it in while working on another job.

We packed the truck and trailer on Sunday, then left Monday morning for the 14-hour drive. At 7 p.m we reached Frederick, Maryland, and stopped for dinner at a Mexican restaurant, hoping that commuter traffic would die down before we headed into the greater metro area.

By the time we arrived at our motel we were exhausted and sore from sitting so many hours. We parked, got our key, and headed to our room. We had agreed to share rooms on the trip, because the budget would not cover separate accommodations. I wondered what kind of relationship the motel clerk imagined we had, a 45-year-old woman with a man of 28. Was I his mother? His much-older girlfriend?

What I really wanted after eating nearly a whole basket of salty tortilla chips was a drink of water. I threw my suitcase on the bed and walked over to the dresser to grab a plastic cup. I was pulling the cup out of its wrapper when I felt something cold and wet: a wad of semen.

"EW!" I screamed, watching the blob stretch into a film when I opened up my hand.

"GO AND WASH YOUR HANDS IMMEDIATELY," Daniel ordered, backing as far away from me as he could get.

I had to wonder what tale of perversity lay behind my find. A male housekeeper who got off on the fantasy of provoking horror in an unsuspecting guest? A disgruntled hotel employee determined to destroy his employer's business?

Facing the prospect of getting up early and finding our way through city traffic to our clients' house, I was ready for bed. Daniel, on the other hand, was itching to explore the local night life. He set off on foot while I settled in.

I was fast asleep when he returned just after 1 a.m. and switched on the light. "*WHAT THE HELL ARE YOU DOING?*" I yelled. I'd been dogged by intermittent insomnia for months and knew there was little chance I'd be able to doze off again.

"Sorry," he said. "I'll turn it off. But how will I be able to find the bathroom?"

"I don't know. Just feel your way. Or go to bed when I do. But don't

EVER turn the light on again after I've gone to sleep."

The next morning we parked in the alley behind our clients' house and carried everything inside. We set up our tools and equipment on the front porch, then left to drop off the trailer at the nearest U-Haul location. No sooner had we returned to the jobsite than the rains descended. From that point on, every day was a steam bath.

I had no intention of going back to that first motel, however handy its location. As we neared the end of our first day I asked our customer if she could recommend someplace affordable nearby. "I always use priceline.com," she said. "I'll book you a room for the night." A couple of hours later she gave us a printout with directions. She'd booked us a room at a Sheraton for less than we'd paid to stay at the Semen Arms.[2]

For the rest of our trip we relied on Priceline. The only catch: We had to wait until after 5 p.m., then choose from whatever might be available. This meant moving our luggage every morning because there was no way of knowing where we'd end up. But what we lacked in geographic stability we made up for in luxurious accommodations most nights. We did feel a bit guilty for lowering standards when we found ourselves, aching, exhausted, and covered in a thin paste of sawdust and sweat, sharing an elevator with guests who were dressed up for an evening on the town.

It's not that our work was especially hard. But besides being hot and dusty, our typical installation requires a blend of brute strength and obsessive attention to detail that keeps me, at least, in a state of high anxiety. Out-of-town jobs are especially nerve-racking because you don't have access to your own shop. You never know when you might need a tool you didn't think to bring. Improvisation is the name of the game. One minute you're lying on the floor in a position you last held while playing Twister at the age of 6, trying to insert the final tiny screw in a drawer slide at the back of a cabinet. The next, you're lifting a 150-pound cast iron sink into place, only to find that the hole you cut out of the counter needs to be enlarged on one side by 1/16".

And then there's the mental end of the stress spectrum: You're constantly figuring out how to solve problems. The morning starts with interpreting installation instructions for various built-in appliances, a literary

---

[1] Credit for the name goes to Daniel.

genre populated by writers for whom English is typically a (distant) second language. "Thred condensate hose into cabinet at Point C. Warning: Be certin not to make a blockage. After applying clamp (Part #37) join hose to rear output flange." Later in the day you're trimming a 9' cherry counter to length on the front porch as rain falls in sheets a mere 3' from your portable workbench when you find, to your horror, that your cut happened to bisect the pressed-wood splines you inserted between the planks to keep them level during glue-up. There's nothing like a nice bit of decorative inlay to remedy such SNAFUs.

Much of this takes place while you are being watched by customers who appreciate your labor as a kind of reality/performance art. "Careful!" they call helpfully, seeing that you're about to set some sharp object on the newly finished hardwood floor. "Watch that hand-painted glass lampshade!"

The best part of each day was lunch. Given our inflexible deadline, there was no telling how late we might have to work into the evening, so we made lunch our main meal. We'd work the first few hours until we reached a logical breaking point, then get in the truck and drive off in search of someplace Indian or Thai. Renewed by good food, air conditioning, and strong coffee, we'd work into the evening as necessary. After a quick nap and shower, Daniel went out for a few hours while I caught up on mail, bathed, and went to sleep.

The bathrooms at the high-end hotels were a blessing, with gleaming floors, endless hot water, and the kind of lighting that makes your wrinkles disappear. There was usually a gracious selection of soaps and shampoos, gels, and lotions.

"You work hard," read an embossed card placed on the marble counter beside the hand-blown-glass vessel sink at one such establishment where we stayed.

> Welcome to your reward at day's end. Lose yourself in a heavenly froth of organic lavender and lemon verbena. Feel those stresses melt away as our artisan-blended shower gel soothes your spirit while gently cleaning your body. To finish, quench your skin's thirst with our mint- and rose-infused balm.

"Wow," I said to Daniel as he buttoned up a fresh shirt, preparing to head out for the evening. "I wonder how many of the people who stay in this place appreciate this stuff as much as we do."

Two nights before the end of our trip we were at a hotel that had a laundry room on each floor. By this time I was out of clean clothes, so I took the opportunity to use the facilities while Daniel went out for dinner.

After nearly two weeks of rifling through my suitcase beneath a burgeoning plastic grocery bag of dirty clothes to seek the remaining unworn underwear and socks, it was a pleasure to gather my warm, sweet-smelling laundry from the dryer and pile it into a basket. I carried the basket back to our room, set it on my bed, and immersed myself in the sensual delight of folding. We were almost done with the job. Things had gone better than I'd had a right to expect, and even though Daniel and I had wanted to kill each other on several occasions, we'd also formed a closer bond. I felt a sense of good fortune and satisfaction as I packed my clothes neatly into my suitcase.

The next day we completed our installation. We spent a couple of hours cleaning the jobsite, carried our tools and equipment across the street, and loaded them into the truck. Amy and Martin had turned out to be wonderful clients: interested in their house's history, actively involved in the remodeling process, and willing to invest in high-quality cabinets, appliances, and counters. Their 1-year-old son was a joy. We bid one another a genuinely fond goodbye as we prepared to drive off.

One of the catches with online booking services is that if you're unfamiliar with a city and don't have time to research a hotel's surroundings, you never really know what kind of area you'll end up in until you get there. Press "book" and you're committed. On that last night of our trip the hotel turned out to be outside the Beltway; glancing at the map, I figured it was one of those locations with no restaurants or shops around. Darkness fell as we crept along the interstate for over an hour in a torrential downpour. When we finally reached our exit I found a shopping center with a sign for a Chinese restaurant. I thought we should get something to eat before proceeding to the hotel; neither of us would want to out again in that weather.

I parked the truck as close to the restaurant as I could get. We'd been rushed when checking out that morning; it was our last day, and we had a lot to get done. I'd stuffed my wallet into my suitcase on top of my clothes so we could leave for work without delay. Daniel had paid for lunch; I would reimburse him later. But now I wanted to get my wallet. I didn't want him to have to front the money for another meal. I jumped out, opened the back door, unzipped my suitcase, pulled the door down, and locked it, rushing to get out of the rain.

We dashed across the flooded parking lot to the Chinese restaurant. A handwritten note taped to the inside of the door said "Closed."

"Well, shit," I said, looking around for alternatives. A fast-food joint sat in the center of the parking lot. Hot, dirty, and now also wet, we didn't feel like walking over on foot, even though it was only a few hundred yards away. "Get back in the truck," I said, and pulled up by the front door.

Aside from us, the place was empty. Ever the good ascetic, Daniel ordered salad. I ordered a baked potato; the weather seemed to demand some kind of comfort food. "Would you like cheese on that?" the server asked. "Sure, why not," I replied, in no mood to worry about calories.

How they get away with calling that cheese I don't know. When I picked up my plastic plate I found the microwave-wrinkled potato drowning in thick, bright-yellow sauce. "Ugh," muttered Daniel. "I can't believe you're actually going to eat something that disgusting." I took my first bite. It wasn't bad. I ate it all. "I will never be able to think about you the same way again," he said.

We climbed back into the steaming truck and turned the air conditioner on full blast to clear the windscreen. "Our last night together," I joked, feigning wistfulness, as we drove off. Neither of us could wait to sleep in our own bed at home and get a break from the other's company.

When we reached the hotel I pulled under the canopy at the entrance, grateful for the shelter from the rain. "I'll stay here," said Daniel as he pulled a biography of Philip Johnson out of his satchel.

"Be right back," I called, slamming the truck door.

A married couple was arguing with the clerk at the reception desk. After 10 minutes I started to think about searching for another hotel. But our reservation could not be cancelled. I couldn't afford to lose the $95 already charged to my VISA card, so I resigned myself to waiting. It was after 9 p.m. What with the downpour, no one in his or her right mind would want to be on the road unless it was absolutely necessary. The line continued to grow; before long, it snaked all the way to the front door. One man walked out, shaking his head. Several others were starting to complain.

After a half-hour, Daniel strode into the lobby. "What the hell is going on?" he asked. I whispered an explanation. He went back out. Another 10 minutes went by before the clerk and the couple at the counter resolved their dispute.

At last it was my turn, a painless matter of the clerk looking up our reservation and handing me a key.

By this time Daniel was in a bad mood and just wanted to lie down in front of the TV. I drove the truck to the side of the building where our room was located. "Give me the key," he said, grabbing his bag and making a dash for the door.

"Great," I thought. It was still pouring. And now I was going to be spending the rest of the evening with a grumpy roommate, through no fault of my own. I opened the driver's-side door, sprinted to the back of the truck, and unlocked it. No less eager than Daniel to get inside for the night, I yanked out my suitcase, only to see my clean clothes fly through the air and land in a filthy puddle. I had forgotten that the zipper was open.

It was perfect, really, I mused, standing in the rain.

Daniel's time with me came to end when his partner completed her doctoral coursework and they returned to Wisconsin. Their move coincided with the start of that devastating economic downturn known as the Great Recession, which would have made it impossible for me to continue employing him. I scarcely had enough work to employ myself. By this time I was in a relationship with Mark, who is now my husband. He invited me to move in with him and rent out my house, thereby saving me from the kind of financial disaster that befell so many.

At first I missed Daniel terribly. I'd spent years working alone before he arrived, but now I felt more alone than ever. There was no one to grouse with about the annoying New Age program on the radio every Wednesday. No one to help me think through technical problems. No one with whom to share my intractable existential anxiety. "You live a life of loud desperation," he'd often said in a twist on the Thoreau quote so close to the truth that it always made me smile.

I missed the way he made me laugh; in fact, my abs were getting soft. I even missed his occasional bad moods. But as time went by, the sense of liberation from the relentless pressure of payroll, worker's comp premiums, and all the other expenses that come with having an employee left me feeling almost light enough to fly.

It's All Problems

Q: WHAT'S THE best piece of advice you ever got from a fellow woodworker?

A: "It's all problems," as my first woodworking employer would say whenever things went wrong. This was in the early 1980s, at a shop in Wisbech, Cambridgeshire. I was 22 and felt overwhelmed whenever things did not go according to plan. I was still laboring under the misconception that if you were good (I mean reasonably good, not necessarily stupendous) at what you did, things would just *work*.

You know how it feels when you're hit by a cascade of small disasters? Your table saw motor dies in the middle of a job for a client who has just changed her mind about yet another critical design element, even though you're halfway through her job and she keeps requesting updates on what she calls "the E.T.A." On the same day, you discover that despite your obsessive habit of measuring not twice, but three times, you've built a pair of doors to the wrong size and are going to have to remake them. You get a call from one of your fellow subcontractors informing you that one of his employees crushed his heel in a fall, as a result of which his work for this deadline-focused client, and now yours, too, will be delayed. The day ends with you opening the mail to find a notice from the sheriff informing you that your business assets are going to be seized because you are delinquent in your corporate tax payment.[1] Naturally all of this happens during a protracted stretch of sweltering, monsoon-worthy weather that makes every challenge feel that much more insurmountable.

---

[1] This happened to me once, thanks to an error by a staff person at the department of revenue. I was not delinquent on any tax payment, but rounding up the necessary paperwork to prove this to the authorities cost me several hours.

When faced with my despondency the first time such an avalanche descended, my boss gave me a little talk about the need to take a more solution-oriented approach to obstacles.

"Come on, you old worrier," Raymond said. "I'll take you out for lunch at the Key Market."

It was a cold, leaden day in the winter of 1981, and our ride through the stalag-like outskirts of town to this mecca of retail just deepened my despair. The Key Market was a monstrous structure that housed a grocery and department store, complete with its own cafeteria. Metal shelves stacked with discount wares towered far above head height, and that was still well short of the ceiling. Fluorescent lights illuminated the vastness with an unearthly glow. It was a surreal, disorienting experience of an alien realm: my first introduction to the now-ubiquitous big box store.

We were not there to shop. We were there for the serious business of setting people straight vis-à-vis priorities and expectations in the world of professional cabinetmaking. We got our plastic trays and proceeded to the food.

In those days I did not go out for lunch. Ever. Who could afford to go out, even to the Key Market? I brought my own lunch to work: either a 5-ounce container of cottage cheese or a sandwich made on one slice of homemade whole wheat bread with four paper-thin slices of cheddar – no butter or mayonnaise – always followed by an apple. I was in my borderline-anorexic phase, so even though I was commuting four miles each way on my bike, my greatest concern aside from the possibility of nuclear war was that I would gain a pound.

I surveyed the options. Beef stew. Steak and kidney pudding. Battered cod with chips. Shepherd's pie with mushy peas. Bangers and mash. Hearty fare for working folk. The sole offering for vegetarians was salad, this being a euphemism for a melamine bowl with three leaves of limp lettuce over which someone had strewn a few wedges of unripe tomato and some cucumber slices just beginning to curl at their edges. The dressing on offer was salad cream, a sweetened mayonnaise thinned down with malt vinegar.

"May I have the salad, please?" I asked.

We carried our trays over to a gray laminate table by the window, which offered an unapologetic view of the dark gray parking lot beneath the light gray sky. I was grateful to have the undivided attention of my boss, who seemed concerned about how low my spirits had sunk in response to the recent series of calamities in the shop. Now, I felt sure, he would share the secret to his confidence and unwavering determination. I was all ears: Grasshopper to my own Shaolin master.

"Look," he said, putting down his fork after a bite of cod. "There's something you've got to understand if you're going to get anywhere: *It's all problems*. That's what we do: solve problems."

That was it?

Still, over the years I've found perverse comfort in Raymond's dictum.

Take the bathroom I did for Andrew, my first job during my short-lived experiment as an aspiring restoration contractor. As part of that project I replaced his old pink toilet with a new white one. The only catch (aside from the fact that this was my first-ever toilet installation): 1.6-gallon-per-flush toilet technology was cutting edge (translation: still decidedly imperfect).

One evening the phone rang as I was reading in bed. "Nancy, it's Andrew," he said. "This is a little embarrassing, I'm afraid. The toilet's plugged."

"I'll be over first thing," I replied, anticipating a sleepless night.

The next morning I stopped by the hardware store to get a plunger.

"Suck or blow?" asked the clerk, Tom, with a deadpan expression. He could get away with being mildly suggestive because we'd been on a couple of dates: the first to Chi Chi's (his suggestion), the next to a locally owned brewpub (mine). It became clear to us both that the latter would be our last when the waiter asked whether I'd like a second beer. "Only a lush has more than one, Nancy," said my date. With that patently ridiculous gauntlet thrown down, I obviously had to order a second.

"*Blow?*" I asked, back in the hardware store. "I didn't know that was even possible."

"Yes, we have plungers of both kinds these days. And both are surprisingly effective."

"Suck," I decided, afraid that any attempt to force a school bus through an opening designed for a Yugo was destined to end badly.

"You might want to take some Altoids to your jobsite," he added as he rang up my purchase. "Plumbers swear by them."

Two days later Andrew called me back. "Toilet's plugged again." This time there was no genteel acknowledgement of the situation's awkwardness. As far as he was concerned, the blockage was the result of my incompetence.

"It's all problems," I told myself.

"Look, I can't have this happen every few days," he said when I arrived. "I'd like you to take the new toilet out and put back the old one."

After clearing out the toilet (Dear Reader: Please pause a moment and allow your imagination to conjure what these easily read five words connote), I took it apart and carried it outside. The old pink commode was still sitting at the end of the driveway, where I had put it when I first took it out. Now I carried it back in – stool in one trip, tank in another – and installed it with a stacked pair of new wax rings, a trick shared by a plumber. I checked that it was working and left.

Another day, another call. "Toilet's *leaking* now. There's water all over the floor."

I suspected the wax was the culprit; I must not have seated the base of the stool correctly. Once again I unscrewed the nuts, pulled the stool, and scraped up the wax with a putty knife. By this time I knew better than to visit Andrew's house without my plumbing tools and some spare wax rings, so I went and got them from my truck. I screwed the thing back down and left.

Lo, the following morning brought yet another summons. "Toilet's still leaking."

Time to hire a pro.

The plumber arrived and made a thorough inspection of my work. "It's not coming from the wax ring," he said. Nor was the leak at the joint between the tank and the stool. No, after intimately inspecting the base of the stool he announced that he'd found a tiny crack in the porcelain. I was confident that I hadn't caused it: I hadn't dropped the toilet during either of the moves, and I'd been careful to avoid over-tightening the nuts. I relayed the news to Andrew.

"Oh dear," he replied, chagrined. "I guess I shouldn't have been bumping into the toilet with my fender these past few weeks. I was using it to indicate when I reached my parking spot."

The plumber assured us that there was no reliable fix; the toilet would have to be replaced. So Andrew asked me to get the 5-gallons-per-flush model from the basement and put the useless new one down there instead. At least the new bathroom now had a white commode.

Then there was a cabinet job I did a decade after Andrew's bathroom. This one took place amid a serious romantic break-up, a time of such emotional pain that my entire being throbbed like a just-hammered thumb.

IT'S ALL PROBLEMS

My clients had been referred to me by a mutual friend who knows I love to work with salvaged materials. They had a treasure trove of leaded glass windows, architectural doors, Vitrolite tile, and hardware salvaged from a family home that had been demolished. My task was to design, build, and install a set of practical cabinets that would incorporate the salvage and evoke an industrial-rustic vibe.

A few months earlier I had moved into the house at my shop property. I was spending all my spare time finishing the interior: laying the hickory floors, making and installing the trim for doors and windows, building cabinets, painting. Daniel was working with me by day, but as soon as he and his cast of entertaining alter-egos left for the night I felt emotionally bereft.

Most people know better than to call a business after hours. You just end up talking to an answering machine, which is fine if all you're going to do is ask the person at the other end to call you back but feels kind of stupid when you find yourself entangled in a message of Proustian complexity. That didn't stop this client.

It was after midnight and I was fast asleep when the phone rang. That sound in the middle of the night always fills me with dread. Midnight calls tend to mean one of three things: tragedy, emergency, or wrong number.

"Nancy? Did I wake you?"

I recognized my client's voice and felt a momentary surge of relief that at least no one had gone to jail or died.

"Yes, Fred," I replied. "I go to sleep at 10 and don't have a separate business line."

"Well, sorry about that," he said. "But now that you're awake, *WHY* would you have put pull-out shelves in a cabinet that's only sixteen inches deep?"

I detected a tone of indignation.

"With a cabinet that shallow," he went on, "the pull-outs are effectively redundant. You added a lot of expense for no improvement in function."

"Am I dreaming?" I wondered. Surely this conversation was not really happening.

"You said you thought they were a good idea," I reminded him. Only after we ended the call did it occur to me that I should have told him I was going back to sleep and would call him in the morning. "You wanted a place to store large bags of cat food that you could reach easily. You stressed that you were looking for maximum convenience, because the bags are heavy. When I suggested pull-outs, you agreed to them."

He said he had no memory of this discussion and expressed his disappointment with my "design."

"Well, anyway," he concluded, ready to sign off for the night. "I'm sorry I woke you."

I was too distressed to fall back asleep. It wasn't just the sudden awakening, or my shock at how he hadn't skipped a beat between apologizing for waking me and launching into interrogation mode. The most disturbing part was being hit by the realization that no matter how carefully I explained things to a client in an effort to ensure that we were on the same page, we still might not be. It was exasperating enough to face the demise of yet another relationship, despite the strenuous behavioral contortions I'd engaged in to please my former partner. Now I was facing what felt like an equivalent experience of dumbfoundment related to work. Was it ever possible to understand a fellow human being, truly to know someone else? The implications shook me to my core.

The next day I mentioned the call to the general contractor on the job. I was working for the clients directly, not through him, but based on our interactions to date I'd come to see him as a kindred spirit. In fact, I regarded him as something of a mentor: He was an astute businessman as well as an accomplished carpenter.

"Have you ever had a client call you in the middle of the night to question some detail of your work?" I asked.

"No," he replied. "Because I learned a long time ago that it's essential to have a separate phone line for my business."

"Fine for you," I thought. Not only did he have his act so much more together than I did, he also had a wife whose job provided their household with a second income. I couldn't afford more than one phone line. Still, he offered some perspective and advice.

"Nancy, they were probably well through a bottle of wine – I'm sure it was a great red – and sitting on the floor in their unfinished kitchen, just beginning to look at the progress with a more critical eye. In the future, send your clients a memo whenever there's a change or addition to the design. That way you'll have proof that they agreed to it."

Another year, another kitchen. Once again I was silently reciting Raymond's dictum like a rosary.

This time the job was for an interior designer. I'll call him Bennet. Well into a successful career, he was ready to have his house remodeled extensively and hired my company to build and install his cabinets.

Bennet's plan would make ingenious use of his limited square footage and transform a dark, cave-like kitchen into one that would feel spacious and be filled with natural light. The cabinets would be made in the contemporary take on modernist style that has since become the standard in minimalist fare. Doors and drawer faces would be veneered; we would arrange these elements with close margins, the grain running continuously between them.

Daniel built the casework that fall. Along the way, Bennet made various design refinements on the fly: an extra cabinet here, a reconfiguration of the oven housing there. A request that we rebuild three upper cabinets when Bennet discovered the doors wouldn't open once the ceiling light fixtures had been installed. Some specialized parts for sculptural components that could only be designed once the majority of the cabinets were in place. Changes to plans are common, but they typically increase costs. Just as important, they prolong the domestic tribulations of those living in a construction zone.

We began installing the cabinets shortly before Thanksgiving, working alongside our client's general contractor and his crew. The kitchen was just one part of a job that encompassed major work around the house. Bennet was adding large windows in his bedroom that would look out on the garden. The laundry room in the basement was going to be enlarged, fitted with customized storage, and get upgraded lighting. There would be extensive repairs to the original siding, with some sections replaced due to woodpecker damage and rot. Then the entire exterior would be repainted.

By the time we arrived, the contractor had put down plastic to protect the floors and completed the interior demolition, leaving a clean slate. Bennet had vacated the kitchen weeks before; he was cooking on an electric skillet perched on a dropcloth-draped sideboard. While the contractor's crew worked in his bedroom, he was camping out in the guest room, across the hallway from the bathroom used by everyone on the job. His bed, dressers, and other bedroom furniture were stacked in a corner of the basement.

We set up a work area in the carport with a portable table saw, chop saw, and workbench, sharing tools with the contractor as necessary to conserve space. November and December were snowy that year. We tramped in and out, up and down the stairs, doing our best to avoid slipping on the ice. Trimming a panel by 1/64" is a special challenge when the temperature's so cold you can scarcely feel your fingers. Sawdust and shavings froze on the piles of snow shoveled to the carport's edges, making it impossible to clean up thoroughly. These conditions are not unusual in our business, but they add a degree of discomfort and inconvenience that can easily translate to stress, especially when you're working to exacting tolerances.

Daniel had just started fitting the doors and drawer faces when he got a call about a family emergency. He would have to take some time off out of town but said he could keep working until the end of that day. He stayed late to finish fitting the doors and drawer faces of a floor-to-ceiling pantry.

The next day I was working on the other side of the kitchen when my eye was caught by the grain on the pantry cabinet. The top drawer was out of alignment with the doors above. The grain was relatively subtle, so the disrupted pattern wasn't glaringly obvious. But there was clearly something amiss.

I unscrewed the drawer face, thinking it had probably been put on upside-down. The grain didn't line up that way, either. I turned it over and realized that Daniel, understandably distracted by his family emergency, had reversed the drawer face, putting the back of the panel outward. Four screw holes gaped on the face. We were already over budget – in part because of changes to the plan, but also because the exotic veneer had proved maddeningly brittle, necessitating what would previously have struck me as an inconceivable number of finicky repairs with cyanoacrylate glue. Now we were behind schedule as well, and things were going to be dragged out further due to Daniel's unavoidable absence.

Bennet, who happened to be going through a romantic break-up during this tumult, was beginning to chafe at the ever-receding horizon. If I redid the veneer on one drawer face, I'd have to redo all the other pantry doors and drawers to make the grain line up. That would add several more days. We had already reached the point where every additional day meant additional torment for Bennet (and so, for all of us on the job). He was clearly reaching the end of his rope, silk tie, and llama-print pajamas. His snippy demeanor whenever our paths crossed was interfering with my ability to sleep, I'd lie awake for hours silently estimating how much longer our part of the job was likely to take. By this time it was clear to us all that every part of this project, interior and exterior, was going to end up well over budget. When my ~~employee~~ mental health coach left to tend to his family, my insomnia flew off the charts. Benadryl, a boon for occasional sleeplessness, no longer cut it. My doctor prescribed a sleep medication, which helped. But as the job wore on I had to double the dose to see any effect. (Ordinarily a small crumb of this medication would knock me out like a light.)

I recalled a visit years before to a friend who worked at an upscale custom furniture shop in Massachusetts. He'd introduced me to a fellow employee, a finishing specialist whose full-time job consisted of fixing damage so masterfully that the repairs were invisible. I had never heard of such a field. He'd shown me a few examples. The man was a wizard. "OK," I thought. "These little screw holes are nothing some tinted material and graining can't make right." It was a quick fix. I had the drawer face back up in no time.

The next day I arrived to find a flurry of pink and yellow Post-its hanging like Buddhist prayer flags around the kitchen. "Missing shelf," said several scattered across the cabinets. Others noted "Hinges need adjustment." I still had several shelves at the shop, so the fact that some were missing wasn't news to me. Nor had I finished finessing the fit of all the parts. I worked my way around making basic adjustments in an effort to keep Bennet happy, aware that still more would be needed before the job was complete.

Once I had fitted the doors and drawer faces I took them back to the shop for finishing. A few days later, when everything was dry, I returned to the jobsite and began screwing it all into place, tweaking to the best of my ability before installing set screws in the hardware. You might imagine that full-overlay doors and drawer faces make for the simplest-possible installation. They do – when these elements have enough space between them to make any inconsistencies in the margins unnoticeable. In this case the margins were 3/32"; any deviation from parallel was magnified to a *Spinal Tap* 11. At the same time, each adjustment of one door or drawer in any of its three planes affected every other one nearby. Not only did the margins need to be consistent, parts in such close proximity must also be in plane. For example, if the right edge of one drawer protruded even just a *little* relative to its neighbor, the neighbor, too, had to be adjusted. Of course, that neighbor would have other neighbors. This scenario results in a ripple effect so far-reaching that I've come to think of such cabinetry as an excellent example of the Buddhist doctrine of dependent origination. Even with adjustable European hardware it can take hours to get a 12' run of cabinet doors and drawer faces aligned. The challenge is only intensified when the grain runs continuously between the parts.

In the midst of this work I was halfway up a ladder between the pantry and oven housing, easing one of the tall pantry doors onto its trio of hinges, when the contractor called my name. Distracted, I turned my head slightly to hear him better and lost my grip on the door. I watched it clatter in slow motion against the pristine stainless steel door of the brand new, very expensive built-in oven.

"No," I thought. "This cannot be happening."

I stepped off the ladder to assess the damage. Miraculously, the cabinet door was barely scathed; it had just one small bruise in an edge that I could easily repair by swelling the wood fibers back into shape with a damp towel and an iron. But the oven door was dented.

I called the appliance company and arranged to buy a new door. I would also cover the cost of having it installed professionally, because the contractor said he was familiar with that particular oven and the door would be a bitch to replace.

I left that evening, expecting to complete my part of the job by lunchtime the following day.

The next morning I was greeted by another swarm of Post-its. "Drawer needs adjustment." "Door needs additional bumper." "Shelf supports sticking. Please fix." And so on. The harmless self-adhesive note had come to feel as menacing as a crow in Alfred Hitchcock's hands. Would Bennet ever be satisfied?

Daniel ended up having to stay in Milwaukee through the completion of Bennet's job. When I figured up the final invoice, I gave Bennet a credit of more than $1,000 because I felt so bad about our part in the delay. An envelope arrived with his payment. Stuck to the check was a pink Post-it on which he'd written "HOW DID THIS JOB GET SO EXPENSIVE???"

Between my work-induced insomnia and Post-it traumatic stress disorder, not to mention my ongoing fear lest I find myself someday working again for the likes of the Billingsworths – clients driven to sabotage their own project – I decided it might be time to close my business and find some less emotionally fraught way to make a living.

I loved much about my work, beginning with the wood itself: ash, whose creamy paleness always brought Gregor to mind; cherry, with its fruity perfume; elm, which smells like a barnyard; the radiant flakes of quartersawn oak; the flame of curly cherry. There's a deep sense of agency that comes from knowing how to design things, then materialize them as functional objects in three dimensions, a sense of self-sufficiency in being able to furnish your own home (even if doing so takes some of us decades; the cobbler's children rarely have shoes). There are my clients, many of whom, including Fred and Bennet, have gone on to become dear friends. There are the contractors and suppliers: Kerry, the lumber deliveryman who, on hearing that my 15-year-old stepson had died, asked if he could take my hand and say a prayer for our family; Calvin, who once sidled up to a box of fresh doughnuts and asked whether I thought Michelle Obama would mind if he ate one.

There's the beauty of the finished work. You return to a client's house years later and find yourself wondering "Did I really build that?" Nothing banishes self-doubt more effectively than objective proof of skill. There's the gratification of knowing that your work is enhancing daily life for your clients. "I need to tell you that every single day I enjoy so much of your work," wrote Alex, one of my longest-standing clients. "I am surrounded by it here in Chicago: the floating bookshelves, the Irwin Miller homage. And when we toggle back to Bloomington, my favorite room is the kitchen. Your work makes our lives work. Not only is it more beautiful, but it gives me so much pleasure to know that you made these things, bleeding knuckles, curses, joy and all."

Who would I even *be* if I were no longer a cabinetmaker? I had lived with that identity for most of my working life, and it had come with a price – not just in terms of low income, but how I'd often been perceived. The trades have not always been viewed with the respect they are earning today. Before Viscount Linley, Queen Elizabeth's nephew, became a furniture maker, an awful lot of people in England looked down on those of us who worked with our hands. That disdain is still surprisingly prevalent in the United States. Perversely, a sort of opposite effect also obtains: Being a painter, plumber, or cabinetmaker with training in classical languages and a master's in religious studies brands you as a weirdo, though that, too, is changing as more and more of us who have spent years in academic study turn to the trades.

What would it mean to go back to an office in my mid-40s – assuming that I was lucky enough to find a job? Sure, the contractors and materials suppliers would remain acquaintances. But I would no longer be part of their world. I would still make furniture and cabinetry in my spare time, but my basic sense of who I was would no longer be bound up with that work.

And yet, was the income – modest in even my best years – really worth the gut-wrenching stress that a few of those jobs had entailed? ("If you have to ask the question, you probably know the answer already" does not apply here.) My doctor had encouraged me to find another line of work due to asthma and scoliosis, both inherited conditions. Perhaps it was time?

I scheduled a meeting with a group of SCORE volunteers to discuss what would be involved in closing the business. They looked at the numbers and listened to my concerns.

"We don't mean to insult you, Ms. Hiller, but you're fooling yourself if you think that this undercapitalized, seat-of-the-pants operation even qualifies as a 'business.' Why would anyone work so hard for less than many clerical workers at the university make?"

This is what I expected to hear.

The words that actually reached my ears were: "Looks like you have a pretty successful business."

"Obviously you're joking," I responded. For once in my life I was not going to fall for that kind of irony. "Look at my income."

"Do you make enough to live on?" he asked.

"Most of the time. But my income is so uncertain. I might well have gone bankrupt and lost my house and shop during the recession if I hadn't had a boyfriend who invited me to move in with him and share expenses."

"You're clearly able to prioritize in response to adverse conditions. And you're not afraid to take risks. While you're expressing some uncertainty to us, you seem confident in your abilities. If you have some other opportunity staring you in the face and really want to go for it, by all means do. But I'm not really sure why you're even here."

This meeting was the Omega to Raymond's Alpha at the Key Market: *Age quod agis*. Simple advice, but sometimes hard to embrace.

Hence my answer in the Q&A at the start of this tale. Perhaps you were expecting something technical: "Invest in a SawStop" or "Tails before pins." With me, it's always more existential. I live in a state of awe – and if you know anything about that word, you're aware that terror is as central as veneration to its meaning. Think of how much we take for granted as we go about our mundane business day by day. Life hangs on the moment-by-moment exchange of gases through a single-cell layer of tissue in our lungs, a process over which we have no control. How do the seams in our trousers, comprised of thread well under a millimeter thick, withstand the stress of kneeling on the floor and getting back up 50 times a day, sitting down at meals, climbing onto counters and crawling under sinks during cabinet installations? Never mind the modern engineering phenomenon of the multi-story garage; it's too easy to envision those structures' collapse in a concrete and steel sandwich. I'm aware that this anxious perspective of mine creates a shaky foundation for everything else I undertake.

I am one of the last people you'd expect to have her own business. My preferred role is that of lieutenant, the trusted partner who provides unflinching commitment and support. Being in charge feels less like a position of power than limitless responsibility.

But looking back I see a subconscious force leading me, in spite of myself, to create the very circumstances that have kept me from doing anything else. Or maybe it's just a series of accidents out of which I've managed to make things work. I am not attached to either explanation.

What Price Authenticity?

"I'M COUNTING the days 'til I can grow back my ponytail," said my old friend Henry one recent Saturday night. Henry and I had known each other since the late 1980s when we worked together one summer for a public-interest research group in rural New England. We'd spent many a happy weekend skinny-dipping in ice-cold swimming holes with Henry's girlfriend, Val.

"I always thought my ponytail was pretty good," recalled my husband. "Then I saw that picture you have of Henry from 1987. Now that was a ponytail."

Now nearing 60, their children grown, Henry and Val (now his wife) were thinking about life post-corporate rat race. They had come to visit us on the occasional Saturday night to escape from their kids, who'd moved home from college for the summer.

We finished dinner and I cleared the table. Henry poured a glass of bourbon and leaned back in his chair. "Ahh," he sighed, closing his eyes in contentment. "I'm starting to become my authentic self again."

This notion of his authentic self had become an increasingly frequent topic of conversation. As far as I could tell, Henry's authentic self appeared to have more in common with the outward trappings of a part he'd play upon retirement than with anything bona fide existential. Far from expressing a lifelong commitment to deeply held values, it was a version of the life he might have lived, had he not parlayed a doctorate in science into a career in chemical weapons research for a company that prefers to be known for its household cleaning products. His income had allowed him to take woodworking classes on weekends and vacations.

"I've become a furniture maker!" he'd announced on their last visit. I wondered what being a furniture maker meant to him. Was it an identity you could simply put on, like a shirt or a coat? Pulling his phone from his pocket, he showed us some photos of a pencil-post bed he'd recently completed. "Hank's part of the Maker Movement!" Val added with gusto.

The bed was handsome, in curly cherry. But I couldn't give the pictures the attention they deserved; my head was spinning as I contemplated Henry's apparent lack of concern over the implication that his entire career – the very livelihood that had enabled him to "become a furniture maker" – had been lived by some other self, one not truly his.

"I think authenticity might entail some sacrifice more substantial than your ponytail," I ventured, aware that I was on dangerous ground. This was, after all, an old friend. But how had this erstwhile reader of Gary Snyder and Edward Abbey managed to get this far in life with such superficial notions about authenticity and the self? No one had forced him to pursue the path he'd taken. He hadn't been imprisoned in a concentration camp, having to choose between sacrificing someone else's life or giving up his own. By global standards, he'd had an almost godlike degree of self-determination.

I couldn't help contrasting Henry's take on authenticity to that of my father, who, early on, renounced the vision of 20th-century American success he was raised to pursue – not because he couldn't cut it as a mid-century mad man, but because, as he put it when he poured out his heart to my mother circa 1966, peering over the abyss of leaving his well-paid job in public relations, "I feel like I've been selling my soul." He went on to bushwhack a career as a freelance writer and consultant on travel and place – a field that now has a name: ecotourism – living from contract to contract, and is still working, out of passion as well as economic necessity, in his 80s.

"Well," Val said, "that kind of authenticity is a luxury we could not afford." Whereupon we turned the conversation to lighter matters.

A Note About the Title

SOME OF you may well have opened this book thinking "Seriously? *Another* book/blog/show/magazine/Instagram post about "making?"
    Indeed. It's not my fault that the verb "make" now rivals such monsters as "awesome" and "curate" for triteness. I started this project before making (let alone talking and writing about it) was not just a thing, but apparently *the* thing.
    The title came to me in 2005, when my erstwhile employee, Daniel O'Grady, and I were installing a set of kitchen cabinets. Our clients had ordered a massive farmhouse-style sink – well, more of a cattle trough, really. "Mark my words," the general contractor said in a private aside. "These guys are going to be partying in that sink. So make sure you give it plenty of support."
    This was the first farmhouse sink I'd encountered. It was not the "apron" type, which has a front panel that overlaps the sink cabinet's face frame. Those are easier to install. No, this one was the more authentic variety, i.e. your cabinet had to be cut out at the sides if you wanted to avoid a gap resulting from the curve of the cattle trough sink at the cabinet's square corners. Such high-end fixtures often arrive with no template or instructions, the expectation apparently being that anyone installing them will be the kind of person who just automatically knows what to do.
    I am not that person.
    "How do *you* figure out how much to cut out of the face frame?" I asked the contractor on the job.
    "Measure very carefully," he says, "make a paper pattern, and cut a little

at a time."

I did. And when we carefully lowered the behemoth into position, we found that my conservative first pair of cuts had already removed too much material.

"*Shh!* Not a word," I whispered to Daniel. "Let's pull the sink back out."

We put the sink back in its box and I pawed through the trash until I found the corner cut-outs. "We're taking this thing home again."

We were easing our way out of the kitchen with the unwieldy cabinet slung between us when one of our clients happened to stop by. "Just taking this one back to the shop to make an adjustment," I reported, as though this kind of thing were par for the course. (I am happy to say it's not.) Meanwhile I was in a cold sweat as I wondered whether I'd be able to fix the cabinet or would have to build a new one.

Once we'd manhandled the thing through the shop door I held each piece of corner waste up to the spot it had come from. The cuts were clean; the pieces still fit. I glued them back and touched up the finish. The fix was invisible and structurally sound.

"Now that's what I call making things work," I told Daniel. "I'm going to write a book by that name."

In the years since that day I worked on this project for extended periods, then put it away, sometimes for a year or more at a time. The book started out as a serious discussion, primarily economic in perspective, about what goes into made things – especially those so common that we tend to take them, along with the materials and lives that go into their production, for granted. As a cabinetmaker with an academic background in classics and ethics, I am most familiar with exposition, analysis, and polemic. But as time went on I decided that some of the points I wanted to make might be better made through anecdotes that leave the reader to find the moral of the story. I recycled all the pages written in more obviously philosophical style.

The notion to make this a humorous book came in the course of my work for another kitchen, the most vexing job of my career. It was only by appreciating the absurdity of the unfolding situation that I was able to get through it.

Since I started this project, several books on related subjects have been published, most notably Matthew Crawford's *Shop Class as Soulcraft: An Inquiry into the Value of Work* (2009), Chris Schwarz's *The Anarchist's Tool Chest* (2011), Peter Korn's *Why We Make Things and Why It Matters: The*

Education of a Craftsman (2013), and Paul Downs's *Boss Life: Surviving My Own Small Business* (2015). Each one is a treasure. I have not yet read the most recent related works that I'm aware of, Nina Maclaughlin's *Hammer Head: The Making of a Carpenter* (2015), and Nick Offerman's *Good Clean Fun: Misadventures in Sawdust at Offerman Woodshop* (2016), though they are on my reading list.

Also by Nancy R. Hiller

The Hoosier Cabinet in Kitchen History (Indiana University Press, 2009)

"Nancy Hiller has produced a book that is as much a small gem of American social and cultural history as it is the history of a product or (less so) of a company."
– John Luke, *American Bungalow*

A Home of Her Own (Indiana University Press, 2011)

"A wolf in sheep's clothing – Betty Friedan disguised as Martha Stewart – *A Home of Her Own* is a set of radical tales of female empowerment posing as a diversion for ladies who lunch."
– Yael Ksander, WFIU Artworks